THE MOST BEAUTIFUL AMONG THE CHILDREN OF MEN.

MEDITATIONS UPON THE LIFE OF OUR LORD JESUS CHRIST.

BY

MRS. ABEL RAM.

WITH A PREFACE BY THE CARDINAL ARCH-BISHOP OF WESTMINSTER.

Copyright © 2018 Read Books Ltd.
This book is copyright and may not be
reproduced or copied in any way without
the express permission of the publisher in writing

British Library Cataloguing-in-Publication Data
A catalogue record for this book is available from
the British Library

PREFACE.

THE following pages were written by a mother who has carefully trained her child from an early age to meditate on Holy Scripture.

What illustrations are to the Bible, and sacred pictures to the Way of the Cross and to the Mysteries of the Rosary—that is to say, vivid representations speaking to the soul through the eye—such are these descriptive meditations speaking to the soul through the ear. They show great care and truthfulness, first in apprehending, and then in presenting to the intelligence and to the heart of children, the life and actions of Our Divine Lord, and the mysteries of the Catholic Faith. Such mental delineations of sacred truths once vividly realized in childhood remain for ever.

There are few who do not owe the light, strength, and guidance, which has helped them in critical moments of their life, to a word of warning, or to a vision of eternity impressed upon them in childhood—the spring time when the wise sower sows his seed.

HENRY EDWARD,
Cardinal Archbishop.

CONTENTS.

	PAGE
Introductory Letter	8
1. The Annunciation	11
2. The Visitation	14
3. Bethlehem.—Birth of Jesus	17
4. Bethlehem.—The Manger	20
5. Gloria in Excelsis Deo	23
6. The Infant God	26
7. The Star in the East	29
8. Adoration of the Magi	32
9. Presentation in the Temple (I.)	35
10. Presentation in the Temple (II.)	38
11. Flight into Egypt	41
12. The Desert	44
13. Night in the Desert	47
14. Arrival in Egypt	50
15. Sojourn in Egypt	53
16. Return to Palestine	56
17. Nazareth	59
18. The Holy Family go up to Jerusalem	62
19. Loss of Jesus	65
20. Finding of Jesus	68
21. Life at Nazareth	71

Contents.

	PAGE
22. Jesus and Mary	74
23. Jesus leaves Nazareth	77
24. Baptism of Jesus	80
25. Jesus goes up into the Wilderness	83
26. Jesus begins to call His disciples	86
27. Marriage at Cana	89
28. Lake of Gennesareth	92
29. Jesus works many Miracles	95
30. Cure of a Leper	98
31. The call of Matthew	101
32. Miraculous draught of Fishes	104
33. Jesus casts the sellers out of the Temple	107
34. Mary Magdalen	110
35. The Woman of Samaria	113
36. The Ruler's child, and the Centurion's servant	116
37. The Widow of Naim	119
38. Kindness of Jesus	122
39. Jesus stills the Tempest	125
40. The Daughter of Jairus	128
41. Choice of the Apostles	131
42. The Twelve Apostles	134
43. Jesus and the Apostles	137
44. The Pond of Bethsaida	140
45. Jesus is followed by a Multitude	143
46. Jesus feeds Five Thousand	146
47. Jesus walks upon the Sea	149
48. Mount Tabor	152
49. Martha and Mary	155
50. Feast of Tabernacles	158
51. Two Blind Men	161
52. Death of Lazarus	164
53. Resurrection of Lazarus	167

Contents.

		PAGE
54. Jesus rides into Jerusalem upon a Colt	.	170
55. Hosanna!	.	173
56. The Cenacle	.	176
57. Jesus washes the Disciples' feet	.	179
58. The Last Supper	.	182
59. The Agony in the Garden	.	185
60. Jesus is taken Prisoner	.	188
61. Humiliations of Jesus	.	191
62. Denial of Peter	.	194
63. Scourging of Jesus	.	197
64. The Crowning with Thorns	.	200
65. Jesus goes to Calvary	.	203
66. Jesus meets His Mother	.	206
67. The Crucifixion	.	209
68. The taking down from the Cross	.	212
69. Mater Desolata	.	215
70. Alleluia!	.	218
71. Ascension of Our Blessed Lord	.	221

Madame et chère fille en Notre Seigneur,

Je suis heureux de vous dire quelle douce emotion j'ai ressentie à la lecture de vos petites méditations. C'est simple sans mièvrerie ; c'est pieux sans prétentions. Il était difficile de mettre l'Evangile à la portée des enfants par un commentaire plus court, plus vivant, plus en harmonie avec les facultés et les goûts de l'enfance ; un tableau qui parle, une vérité sortant d'elle-même du texte sacré, un bon mouvement du cœur, une aspiration vers le bien, le beau, le divin ; tout cela en quelques lignes qui ont le charme, la douceur, la suavité de la voix d'une mère à l'oreille de son fils, voilà votre livre.

Pour trouver cet accent qui va au cœur il faut être mère, et aimer les enfants comme Jésus les aimait. Les mères chrétiennes goûteront ce petit ouvrage, et seront heureuses de pouvoir initier les jeunes gens confiés à leur tendresse, grâce à cette lecture d'un style si simple et si pénétrant, au double amour de la parole de Dieu et de la méditation.

C'est au moins le succès qui je souhaite et la bénédiction qui j'envoie à votre petit livre, en vous renouvelant, Madame et chère fille en Notre Seigneur, l'hommage de mon plus respectueux dévouement.

Fr. Bernard Chocarne,
des Frères Prêcheurs.

Flavigny, Octobre, 1883.

My dear Daughter in Christ,
   I cannot tell you with what pleasure I have read your little book of meditations. It is simple without affectation, devotional without being pretentious. It would be difficult to place the Gospels before the comprehension of young minds by a commentary more vivid, concise, and in harmony with the tastes and faculties of youth ; a picture which speaks, a truth springing spontaneously from the sacred text, a good impulse of the heart, an aspiration towards the good, the beautiful, the divine ; all this in a few lines which possess the charm, the sweetness, the gentleness of a mother's voice speaking in the ear of her son : such is your book.
   In order to find these accents which go straight to the heart, one must be a mother and love children as Jesus loved them. Christian mothers will appreciate this little work, and will be glad to initiate the youthful souls entrusted to their tender care into the twofold love of the Word of God and of the practice of meditation by means of these pages, so touchingly and simply written.
   Such is, at any rate, the success which I wish and the blessing I send to your little book.
      Br. Bernard Chocarne, O.P.

Flavigny, October, 1883.

THE ANNUNCIATION.

"And in the sixth month the Angel Gabriel was sent from God into a city of Galilee, called Nazareth, to a Virgin espoused to a man whose name was Joseph, of the house of David; and the Virgin's name was Mary."—St. Luke i. 26, 27.

INVOCATION.—My God, bless this my meditation, I pray Thee, and give me the grace of devout attention to Thy mysteries.

I. Among the hills of Galilee the sunny little village of Nazareth nestles, hidden amidst vineyards and olive-trees. Half buried under clusters of deep green myrtle bushes, scarlet pomegranates, and fragrant flowering shrubs, I see a modest little dwelling, its white walls glistening in the moonlight. It is Mary's house. I enter the humble doorway, and kneel in spirit at the threshold of the blessed Virgin's chamber.

A fair maiden is kneeling in prayer, her hands meekly clasped upon her bosom, her eyes modestly cast down to the ground. Her lips move, and I fancy I hear her asking God to send His Messias to her people, and to grant that she may be counted worthy to become the humble servant of the Child's Mother.

II. As Mary prays, a soft, heavenly radiance fills the little chamber, more brilliant than the moonshine streaming in through the open lattice. A glorious Angel is standing before the maiden, who salutes her with the words, "Hail, full of grace!" Mary is startled. Who is she, methinks I hear her say to herself, that an Angel should greet her in such language? And Gabriel reassures her gently, bidding her fear not, and telling her that her pure and holy life has made her lovely in the sight of God, and that He has chosen her to be the Mother of His Son.

O Mary, blessed among women! I kneel at thy feet. I kiss the hem of thy robe. I listen for thy response. "Be it done unto me according to thy word," thou sayest, Mother of my Saviour. Permit me to dwell with thee. Permit me to pray beside thee in thy humble chamber. Permit me to serve thee, as thou didst beg to be allowed to serve the Mother of Jesus. Teach me thy virtues, that I also may find favour in the eyes of God by the purity and holiness of my life!

III. The glorious message came to Mary in the stillness of night, as she was kneeling in the solitude of her own chamber, absorbed in fervent prayer. This teaches me that if I would learn to know Jesus, and would win His love and receive His grace, I must *pray*. I must not content myself with a few hurried prayers, almost mechanically said, morning and night; but I must choose a quiet moment, when, alone and undisturbed, I can think of Jesus, invite Him to come into my heart, listen to His sweet voice, and tell Him all my wants, showing Him my poverty, and begging Him to enrich me with His graces.

RESOLUTION.—I will make a practice of saying my vocal prayers aloud when circumstances permit, in order that my attention may be the better sustained. I will make the sign of the Cross devoutly when I awake, and give my heart to Jesus, and before all the principal actions of the day. I will fix upon some special time for making my little meditation, and will be faithful to it every day, asking Mary to help me, and give me holy thoughts and good resolutions.

PRAYER.—Holy Mary, Mother of God, pray for us sinners, now and at the hour of our death.

THE VISITATION.

"And Mary, rising up in those days, went into the hill-country with haste into a city of Juda."—St. Luke i. 39.

INVOCATION.—Mother of beautiful love! I place all my confidence in thee.

I. Far away from Nazareth, in the hill-country, there is a pretty village called Hebron. Its flat-roofed houses slope gently into a valley carpeted with flowers. In one of these houses lives Elizabeth, the cousin of Mary.

I picture her to myself standing, one summer's evening, under a porch covered with trailing roses, whose fragrance fills the air. Shading her eyes with her hand, Elizabeth looks earnestly at the figure of a young girl coming up from the valley. The red tunic, blue mantle, and white veil, tell her whence the unexpected visitor comes, and her heart beats with glad surprise. As the gracious maiden approaches, Elizabeth is inspired by the Holy Ghost, and goes forward to meet her young cousin, with the exclamation, " Blessed art thou amongst women. . . . Whence is this to me that the Mother of my Lord should come to me ?"

II. For nearly three months Mary dwells with Elizabeth, rendering her humble services and tending her with a loving, thoughtful charity; for Elizabeth is advanced in years, and delicate in health.

During those three months, often must the holy cousins have held sweet converse together, seated under the shade of some spreading tree, or wandering, by the clear moonlight, amongst the sweet-scented shrubs in the cool of evening. I can fancy the elder woman listening reverently to Mary's oft-told tale of the Angel Gabriel's visit. The coming of Jesus would be their constant subject. Mary's lips could never tire of repeating His sweet Name, her heart never cease giving praise for the honour of having been chosen as His mother.

Holy Mary! grant that I may kneel at thy side and learn from thee how to bring charity into all my conversation.

If only I could remember that Jesus is listening to every word I say, how different would be my intercourse with others! How often should I keep a discreet silence instead of asking impertinent questions, interrupting others when they are speaking, or, worse still, saying unkind, uncharitable things about my neighbour!

I learn also from Mary's visit to her holy cousin to choose for my intimate friends those only whose lives and conduct are pleasing to Jesus, whose faith is the same as my own, and whose example is beneficial to myself.

RESOLUTION.—I will endeavour to imitate Mary by trying to give pleasure to those whom I visit. For instance, by taking fruit or a bunch of flowers to an invalid, by enlivening the weary hours of poor little sick or infirm children, by reading to them, or amusing them —in fact, by devoting my leisure to rendering any services within my power.

PRAYER.—Holy Mary! help me to sanctify my visits; teach me to speak little and mildly, little and well, little and simply, little and frankly, little and affably, and to offer all my actions to Jesus.

BETHLEHEM.—BIRTH OF JESUS.

" For a *Child* is born to us, and a Son is given to us."
—Is. ix. 6.

INVOCATION.—Holy Mary, teach me to pray to thine Infant Son, I entreat thee; help me to collect my wandering thoughts, and to fix them upon Jesus.

I. The hills and slopes around Bethlehem lie quiet and still in the deep shadows of a December night. The little town itself is all bustle and confusion. Joseph and Mary, way-worn and fatigued, seek hospitality from its churlish inhabitants in vain. The sweet face of Mary is pale. She has been travelling for four long days across the mountains from Nazareth, exposed to wind and rain, cold and frost. Joseph is anxious. Where shall he find shelter for his young wife? Rebuffed by all on account of their poverty-stricken appearance, the humble couple leave the town and enter a cave outside the walls —a gloomy excavation in the rock, already tenanted by an ox and an ass, which turn their large, meek eyes wonderingly upon the new-comers.

II. It is midnight. The Blessed Virgin kneels in prayer, whilst St. Joseph endeavours to make the wretched cavern more habitable, contriving a bed on which Mary may rest, and hanging a sort of screen across the entrance to the cave in order to exclude the chilly night air. Suddenly a brilliant light illumines the cave. Kind St. Joseph, may I enter and contemplate the holy scene?

III. At Mary's feet, bathed in a soft radiance, a little babe is lying upon the ground— a fair, beautiful babe. He trembles with cold, He weeps, and stretches out His tiny arms towards His Mother, as if begging to be taken to her bosom. Mary, her gentle face lit up by joy, and loving, worshipful adoration, lifts Jesus from the ground, presses Him to her heart, and strives to warm Him with her kisses.

I draw near in company with St. Joseph, and, kneeling at Mary's feet, adore my Infant God. Sweet Mother, I pray thee place thy lovely Babe in my arms for a moment, that I may tell Him how much I love Him. I know that this dark cavern is filled with glorious angels, although they are invisible to my eyes. I will join my feeble voice to their songs of praise. I will thank the dear Babe for coming into this miserable world to brighten it by His loveliness. I will ask Him to take my heart and keep it for me, so that I may be His faithful, devoted servant all the rest of my life.

RESOLUTION.—I resolve to take the Divine Infant as the model of all my actions, and I will make a practice of asking myself several times a day, Would Jesus have acted thus? Would Jesus have spoken thus? Am I pleasing Jesus?

PRAYER.—Blessed Mother, by the joy which thou didst feel on first beholding thy Divine Babe, beg of Him, I pray thee, to accept me as His child.

BETHLEHEM.—THE MANGER.

"And she brought forth her first-born Son, and wrapped Him up in swaddling-clothes, and laid Him in a manger; because there was no room for them in the inn."—St. Luke ii. 7.

INVOCATION.—Holy Mary! blessed Joseph! Help me, I pray you, to understand these sacred mysteries.

I. The Divine Babe is sleeping. I draw near to contemplate Him. Mary kneels by His side, gazing upon her Child with looks in which happiness and sadness are mingled. What mother is there who would not grieve at placing her tender infant in such a cradle? A cold stone manger is His bed. A handful of coarse, prickly straw is His pillow. A few poor swaddling-clothes scarce protect His delicate limbs from the cold. My heart is filled with compassion as I behold the holy Infant reduced to such a depth of poverty. He must suffer in so hard a bed! Straw is the customary litter of animals; it is not fit to be the resting-place of a tender Babe! Why cannot I give Thee my heart, sweet Lord? It is hard, I know; it is cold: but surely not so cold as the manger, not so hard as the straw!

Alas! when Jesus comes into my heart in the Blessed Sacrament of His love, does He not too often find it colder than the cold of Bethlehem? My indifference and ingratitude, do they not pierce His tenderness, even as the straw pierced His tender limbs in the manger?

II. Hark! Mary is singing to the little slumberer!* Heaven suspends its music, and angels approach to listen to the strain. "My Babe," the Mother sings, "my God, my beloved, Thou sleepest, and I am dying with love of Thee! Thy closed eye-lids fill me with love. Thy rosy cheeks enchant my heart. Thy sweet lips attract mine!" And the Mother, carried away by her love, snatches her darling to her breast, and imprints a kiss on His Divine features. The Babe awakes, His beautiful face beaming with love; He smiles back into His Mother's eyes.

Can I look upon such a Mother, and such a Son, and not feel my own heart grow warm and tender? I know that the least sacrifice of my own will consoles the heart of the Infant Jesus for the poverty and destitution He is enduring. I know that the offering I make Him of my fastidiousness, of my delicacy,

---

* Hymn of St. Alphonsus Liguori: "Mary contemplating the sleeping Jesus."

when I have some trifling inconvenience to endure, cheers Him in His suffering. I will not refuse Him this consolation.

RESOLUTION.—I will endeavour to please Jesus by preparing my heart for His abode. In place of straw, I will bring Him the flowers He loves best—meekness, charity, and obedience. In place of the damp, hard stone, I will make Him a bed of patience and humility; and instead of the warm breath of the lowly animals, I will bring Him my love with which to comfort His chilled limbs.

PRAYER.—Sweet Infant Jesus! I give Thee my heart. Oh! Mary, take these my resolutions, and offer them to the Holy Child, I entreat thee.

GLORIA IN EXCELSIS DEO.

"And there were in the same country shepherds watching, and keeping the night-watches over their flock. And behold an Angel of the Lord stood by them, and the brightness of God shone round about them, and they feared with a great fear."—St. Luke ii. 8, 9.

INVOCATION.—Holy Infant Jesus, I offer Thee all my thoughts. Show me, I pray Thee, what Thou dost desire of me.

I. The stillness of night is upon the plains of Juda. A little company of shepherds are watching their flocks.

Suddenly a brightness like that of the sun shines around them, and an Angel appears before their startled eyes. They are poor, simple men, these shepherds, more familiar with the face of the silvery moon and the twinkling of the stars than with the habitations of men. They lead a solitary outdoor life, and would seem to have caught some of the quiet, peaceful ways of the meek creatures with which they spend their lives. Their lowliness has attracted the love of Jesus. He calls them, the first to worship at His Crib.

But they are affrighted at the glorious Messenger: their hearts quail for fear.

"Fear not," says the Angel, "for behold I bring you good tidings of great joy. . . . For this day is born to you a Saviour—who is Christ the Lord—in the city of David. And this shall be a sign unto you. You shall find the Infant wrapped in swaddling-clothes and laid in a manger."

II. As these sweet-sounding words die upon the air, a burst of heavenly music peals through the skies and rolls over the mountain tops. The shepherds look upwards, and behold a countless multitude of bright, glorious angels. Spell-bound they gaze, and their hearts melt within them at the wonderful words wafted to their ears on the breezes of the night. "*Gloria in excelsis Deo!*" sing the angelic host; "Glory to God in the highest, and on earth peace to men of good-will!"

Christmas is truly one of the Angels' feasts. The way in which we find these pure spirits ever interwoven with the life of the Infant God shows me that, as praise is their unceasing occupation, so praise should be perpetually on my lips here on earth. But how can I glorify God? I so soon weary of prayer! Scarcely have I asked Our Blessed Lord to give me those things of which I am in need, than I hasten to arise from my knees, forgetting to praise Him for His goodness, forgetting to thank Him for all His gracious answers to my requests. And yet there is no creature on earth, be it ever so small, which was not created for the express purpose of giving glory to God!

"My child," I hear the voice of my Guardian Angel saying to me, "you have a thousand ways in which you can glorify God. You glorify Him when you are obedient to your parents; when you are faithful to your daily duties; when you are amiable towards those around you; and, above all, when you are gentle and forgiving towards those who vex or tease you." "My good Angel, these every-day virtues which sound so easy I find very hard to practise. I make good resolutions, and at the first little vexation or rough word my pride is aroused, and I forget them all!" "My child," continues the Angel, "a *good will* is all that Jesus asks. Never be discouraged, no matter how many are your faults, no matter how hard they be to correct! Only *will*, and Jesus will come to your help! Does he not say 'Fear not'?"

RESOLUTION.—I am determined to *will* henceforth with my whole heart, and when, after many a struggle and many a broken resolution, I fall back into a bad habit, I will turn my thoughts to the dear Infant Jesus, Who chose to become weak and helpless that I might be strong. I will ask Him to give me strength, and then I shall not fear.

PRAYER—Holy Mary! I pray thee be a Mother to me. Save me from falling, and

THE INFANT GOD.

"And it came to pass, after the Angels departed from them into heaven, the shepherds said one to another: Let us go over to Bethlehem. . . . And they came with haste: and they found Mary and Joseph, and the Infant lying in a manger."—St. Luke ii. 15, 16.

INVOCATION.—Behold me at Thy feet, sweet Infant Jesus! I pray Thee grant that I may understand Thy holy teachings.

I. At the sound of footsteps advancing towards the cave in the dead of night, I can fancy St. Joseph, the faithful guardian of the Holy Child, looking out into the darkness, and when he perceives the shepherds approaching, admitting them with a kindly greeting into the presence of Jesus and Mary.

The Babe is lying in the Manger. Mary, on whose countenance rests an indescribable expression of calm, thankful joy, encourages these first worshippers of her Treasure to draw near and adore Him.

The shepherds reverently prostrate themselves before the Child. They are deeply moved at the sight of their Infant Saviour. Their promptitude in obeying the word of the Angel has drawn down upon their souls immense graces of faith and love. Jesus called them, and they obeyed and came, as simply as their sheep would come to their own call. Jesus loves the lowly and the simple, and His little Face beams lovingly on these His first worshippers.

II. And now Mary takes the Holy Infant from the manger, and permits the shepherds to kiss His hands and feet, and look closely into His sweet, loving eyes. Oh, happy shepherds! who would not envy you such joy! Mother Mary, I implore thee give thy sweet Babe into my arms; permit me to press Him tenderly to my heart, that from the depths of those wondrously beautiful eyes I may learn to know His will, and to love those virtues which are so dear to Him!

The glory of heaven has descended into a poor stable. Myriads of angels are adoring a weak, helpless Babe lying in the arms of a poor Jewish maiden. His first worshippers are shepherds. There are great lessons here for me to learn. When I see that, from the very beginning of His life, Jesus chose privations and discomfort for His constant companions—when I behold the lowliness and poverty of His surroundings, I understand that I must imitate Him. I must think less of my own ease than I have hitherto done. I must not esteem people merely because they are rich, nor desire riches myself; and if God sends me wealth, I must not set my heart on it, but use it generously in His service, in helping those poorer than myself, for the sake of Him Who chose poverty for His earthly lot.

RESOLUTION.—When I am inclined to look disdainfully on those who are not so well born as myself, or to despise others on account of their humble condition, I will remember that Jesus called the shepherds, who were poor, to His Crib, before He called the Kings. In memory of the poverty and helplessness of the Babe of Bethlehem, I will be kind and gentle towards little children, and towards all who are neglected or dis-esteemed on account of their poverty.

PRAYER.—Holy Infant Jesus! grant me the grace of a meek and humble spirit, I beseech Thee.

THE STAR IN THE EAST.

"And behold the star which they had seen in the East, went before them, until it came and stood over where the Child was."—St. Matt. ii. 9.

INVOCATION.—Most sweet Infant Jesus, I beseech Thee give me grace to make a holy meditation.

I. I transport myself in spirit to the far East. A group of dark-skinned Oriental sages are studying the skies, the deep blue of which is studded by innumerable stars. Suddenly they perceive a star of unusual shape and brilliancy. Eagerly they consult their learned books. Yes, there can be no doubt! It is the sign they have long looked for—the star which is to lead them to the feet of the newly-born Saviour of the world! Long have they pined for His coming! Night after night have they scanned the skies, longing for the appearance of a sign.

Quickly the three Kings call together their servants and attendants, and announce that they are about to start on a journey. They know not whither they are bound. They know not whether the journey will be long or short. All they know is that the star will guide them to the feet of Jesus: that is enough.

II. The Kings leave their homes and the government of their subjects without a moment's hesitation, confident, in their simple faith, that as God calls them, He will supply their absence. Friends and advisers were not wanting to try and dissuade them from their project, which some blamed as rash and dangerous, others ridiculed as sheer folly. The Kings remained unshaken in their resolve: their faith in God's promises is too strong to be moved by blame, ridicule, or dread of hidden danger.

This prompt departure of the Wise Men contains two lessons for me: in their docility, and their steadfastness of purpose. Like the shepherds, the instant God calls them, they obey the call. They are not simple, uneducated men, but are counted amongst the wisest of the studious East; and they are as obedient to grace, as simple of heart, as the humble shepherds. God often speaks to me by some holy impulse, or by the voice of my conscience prompting me to do a good action. Do I always obey? I am perhaps on the point of obeying, and a word of blame or look of ridicule puts my good resolution to flight, and makes a coward of me! Alas, here is indeed matter for self-examination! If I am thus easily diverted from a good intention, I must be both weak and vain, since it is pride alone which gives me so great a fear of ridicule.

III. I watch the procession as it starts.

The long train of camels and brilliantly attired retinue forms a picturesque caravan as it winds up and down the steep mountain paths, or spreads out majestically across the smooth plains, led by the wondrous star. The dark countenances of the Kings are lit up by joy and hope. They are going to see the Infant God; and neither the perils of an unknown land, nor the fatigues of a long and wearisome journey, have power to wring from them one word of discontent or fear. They push bravely on, their eyes fixed on the star, their hearts fixed on Jesus.

RESOLUTION.—I will strive to follow the example of the Kings, and when I am laughed at for performing some good action, or for obeying the wishes of my superiors, I will no longer stifle the voice of my conscience, as I have, alas! so often done heretofore, and will go bravely on my way, fixing my eyes and my heart on Jesus, regardless of sneers or interference, doing what I know to be right, confident that thus I shall reach the feet of the Holy Infant, and receive one of His sweet smiles in reward for every victory which I shall have gained over my vanity and cowardice.

PRAYER.—Holy Infant! I pray Thee make me strong and brave in Thy service, and grant that my greatest desire may be to please Thee.

ADORATION OF THE MAGI.

" And entering into the house, they found the Child with Mary His Mother, and falling down they adored Him ; and opening their treasures, they offered Him gifts: gold, frankincense, and myrrh."—St. Matt. ii. 11.

INVOCATION.—Holy Child Jesus! I give Thee my heart. I pray Thee bless all my thoughts, desires, and resolutions.

I. I kneel once more beside the Mother of Jesus. Her little Babe is sleeping peacefully in her lap. She gazes at Him, her whole heart absorbed in His loveliness. Suddenly a distant sound is heard, a confused murmur, mingled with the tinkling of bells. It comes nearer and nearer, and exclamations of joy fill the air. Through the opening of the cave I perceive a strange cavalcade approaching. A long line of gaily caparisoned camels draws near; it pauses. The star has ceased its shining, and slowly sinks earthward over the stable of Bethlehem.

II. The three Kings enter the cave, and humbly cast themselves upon their knees; tears of joy and emotion coursing down their bronzed cheeks, as they contemplate the Saviour of the world: a tiny, helpless Babe in the arms of His Mother.

And now the royal worshippers open their

treasures, and pour out their offerings at the feet of the Child. The dark cavern is filled with glittering ingots of ruddy gold; Arabian perfumes of priceless worth shed their fragrance around; whilst the myrrh, symbol of bitterness, costly though it be, is a pathetic prophecy of the path of suffering which lies between the Babe of Bethlehem and His redemption of mankind on Calvary!

III. The Gospel narrative does not tell us how long the kings remained in the cave; it does not mention the holy converse which they would hold with Mary and Joseph—but I can fancy the eager questions which they ask about the Child, the reverence with which they listen to the words which fall from Mary's lips, and the sweet peace which fills their hearts, as they leave the presence of Jesus to carry the glorious news of the Saviour's birth to their distant homes, and win souls to Christ.

Is there nothing, sweet Babe, which I too can bring Thee? Must I come empty-handed to Thy Crib? Alas; I might offer Thee the gold of my love, but it is all tarnished with self-love—no meet present for Thee! I have not the fragrant incense of prayer to give Thee, for my prayers are so short, so distracted, often, alas! so irreverent! I cannot bring Thee the myrrh of mortification, for I am too indolent to overcome my failings, too selfish to forego a gratification for Thy sake! What, then, can I give Thee?

RESOLUTION.—I will take courage from the sweetness of my Infant Saviour, and will bring Him my heart, hard as it is, cold and empty as it is, and ask Him out of the treasures of His love to warm it, soften it, and fill it.

PRAYER.—I beseech Thee, gracious Babe, give me the gold of Thy love, the frankincense of devout recollectedness in prayer, and the myrrh of self-sacrifice—courage to do Thy will at the expense of my own ease and pleasure.

PRESENTATION IN THE TEMPLE. (I.)

" .... They carried Him to Jerusalem, to present Him to the Lord."—St. Luke ii. 22.

INVOCATION.—Holy Infant Jesus! I give Thee my heart and my mind. Make me attentive, I pray Thee, to the teachings of Thy life.

I. Forty days have elapsed since the birth of Jesus. At early dawn on a bright spring morning, the Holy Family are wending their way from Bethlehem to Jerusalem. I follow them in spirit. Mary wraps the folds of her blue mantle round the Babe, to shield Him from the chilliness of the morning air. St. Joseph walks beside her, carrying the modest pair of turtle-doves, with which, according to law, he is going to redeem the first-born son. The Babe rests on His Mother's arm, His eyes looking peacefully out upon His own beautiful world, and on the white terraces and towers of proud Jerusalem, as they glitter in the morning sunlight. To the eyes of the Jewish men and women who pass by and turn a curious look upon the young Mother, He appears to be an ordinary babe.

II. There is, indeed, nothing in the appearance of the Holy Family to attract attention. Mary is, perhaps, more beautiful than are most of the Jewish maidens, for her face is beautiful by her exceeding holiness. It is impossible to watch Jesus continually and not grow to resemble Him; and Saints tell us many sweet things about the likeness between Jesus and His Mother. Joseph wears the dress of an ordinary artisan. If his countenance is noble and dignified, stamped as it is by his saintliness, the crowds who are pushing their way up and down the steps of the Temple, and through the great portico, are too busy to notice it.

I can imagine Mary and Joseph standing meekly aside to let others pass before them. They have no desire to be known, no wish to be noticed. It is enough for them that Jesus is with them; they seek nothing beyond. Oh, my sweet Infant Lord! Teach me Thy humility, I pray Thee! When I see Thee thus choosing poverty for Thy lot, allowing Thyself to pass unobserved, unworshipped in the throng, my conscience tells me how far I am from being like Thee! Thou choosest obscurity, and I am always seeking to be known and admired! I think myself of so much consequence, that if others pass me by without appearing to notice me, I feel hurt and annoyed.

III. The example of the Holy Family teaches me that I must try to pass unnoticed with Jesus, Mary, and Joseph, and surely I need not complain when I am in such sweet company! I must give God thanks for the talents or position which He has given me, but I must never forget that humility and unaffected simplicity are the greatest ornaments to every rank in life, and that the higher my rank, the deeper should be my lowliness of heart; otherwise I shall not be like Jesus, Who was King of Heaven and at the same time the poorest of earthly children.

RESOLUTION.—When I am in the company of others, I will watch myself closely, and whenever I feel inclined to put myself forward, I will make an act of humility, and try to draw attention to the merits of my neighbour. For the love of the Holy Family, I will strive to be more respectful towards my elders, more amiable towards my equals, and kinder to my inferiors than heretofore.

PRAYER.—My sweet Jesus! help me, I pray Thee, to conquer my love of admiration, and give me a great desire of imitating Thee.

PRESENTATION IN THE TEMPLE. (II.)

". . . . They carried Him to Jerusalem, to present Him to the Lord. . . . And to offer a sacrifice according as it is written in the law of the Lord, a pair of turtle-doves, or two young pigeons."—St. Luke ii. 22, 24.

INVOCATION.—Blessed Virgin, help me, I pray thee, to know Jesus better and better, and to love Him more and more.

I. Mary and Joseph have entered the Temple. The courts through which they walk modestly forward, in devout recollection of spirit, are paved with rare marbles; the walls are studded with brilliant mosaics; precious stones and gold and silver gleam and glitter in curiously-wrought designs from pillar and roof. Sweet perfumes, burning in countless censers, fill the atmosphere with soft wreathing clouds of vaporous smoke.

A new worshipper now greets the Holy Family; an aged man named Simeon, who has spent his life in the Temple, trusting that he might see the Messias before he should die. God has granted his prayer. In a transport of joy, he takes the Babe from the arms of His Mother and blesses Him, whilst the thankfulness of his soul finds utterance in a hymn of praise.

II. Meanwhile a second worshipper joins the group. A venerable widow, Anna the Prophetess, worn out by prayer and fasting. She, too, has longed with an intense desire to see the face of Jesus. It is a beautiful and a touching scene which I contemplate in spirit. The child held forth in the arms of Simeon— the long silvery beard of the holy Israelite, and his shrunken, wrinkled features, strangely contrasting with the tiny form, lying like a fair lily upon his arms—the aged prophetess kneeling in speechless adoration and joy before her God; Mary and Joseph standing by, the Mother's eyes fixed upon her Babe.

Oh! sweet Infant Jesus, admit me, I pray Thee, into this little band of saintly worshippers! Cast upon me a look of love. Teach me to long for Thee, and to desire Thee with Simeon and Anna, I beseech Thee.

III. Mary and Joseph are standing before the altar at which first-born sons are offered to the Lord. I picture to myself the high-priest holding the Babe. Mary has given her Child to God. I watch the Holy Infant as He is laid upon the altar beside the two little turtle doves—fitting emblems of the innocence and gentleness of the Child, for Whom they are offered. His lips speak no word, but I can read the thoughts which are passing through His brain, for I know that He is offering Himself, an innocent victim, to God the Father, for me and for the whole world. His eyes say plainly what His lips do not utter: Father, I offer Thee My life, I offer Thee My Blood for the salvation of the world.

If Jesus offers His life to God the Father for love of me, it is only just that I should give Him my life in return.

RESOLUTION.—Henceforth I will make a practice of offering myself to Jesus whenever I hear the clock strike, whenever I leave one room for another, go out, or come in; I will, besides, offer Him my actions and my intentions several times a day, besides my general intention in the morning.

PRAYER.—My Blessed Lord, accept me as Thy child, I beg of Thee. Holy Mary, show thyself a Mother to me, I entreat thee.

FLIGHT INTO EGYPT.

".... An Angel of the Lord appeared in sleep to Joseph, saying : Arise, and take the Child and His Mother, and fly into Egypt : and be there until I shall tell thee : for it will come to pass that Herod will seek the Child to destroy Him."—St. Matt. ii. 13.

INVOCATION.—Holy Child Jesus, grant me to meditate devoutly upon Thy sufferings.

I. Mary and Joseph are returning from Jerusalem, and directing their steps towards Nazareth. It is more than a day's journey. One night, as they are sleeping, an Angel appears to St. Joseph, and tells him that the life of Jesus is in danger, that Herod seeks to kill Him, and that he (Joseph) must fly with the Child and His Mother into the land of Egypt.

How St. Joseph must grieve at this message ! I can fancy him rising quickly from his bed, and gently, tenderly awakening Mary. They are travellers, and have few worldly possessions with them—a few poor garments, perhaps, some carpenter's tools, and one or two of the most ordinary cooking utensils. These Joseph gathers together into a bundle, whilst Mary wakes the Holy Infant. I picture the sweet young Mother to myself, pausing a moment to gaze upon the Divine Slumberer with a mother's natural unwillingness to awaken a child out of his sleep, and then, at the thought of His peril, snatching Him quickly to her bosom and covering Him with caresses. St. Joseph stands waiting at the door, his lantern in his hand; then swiftly, treading lightly and softly, he and the Blessed Virgin with her Babe go forth into the darkness of the night.

II. How heavy and care-oppressed must be their hearts! Every tree and shrub may conceal a lurking danger! They are bound for a strange—a heathen land! They are poor now: there they will be destitute! A thousand anxious fears crowd into their minds. The future looks as dark and impenetrable as the night which lends its cover to their flight.

A glance at the sweet Babe, nestling so peacefully in His Mother's arms, is sufficient, however, to give them courage and confidence. Mary presses Jesus closely to her beating heart, and Joseph walks bravely on, leading the meek, patient ass, on which he has placed the Mother and her Child.

Here is a great lesson for me. In moments of danger I must press Jesus to my heart, and then I need have no fear. Difficulties lose all their terror when Jesus is present. My trials are not very great, it is true, but there are times when my heart is heavy and the future looks black. I feel so weak, I know myself to be wavering, and the very possibility of temptation alarms me!

RESOLUTION.—At such moments as these, and when I feel weary of struggling to do right, tired of obeying, tired of working, tired of keeping my temper under provocation, inclined to follow a bad example, or otherwise give way to temptation, I will go to my room, or to some quiet spot, and, kneeling down, ask Our Lady to place her Holy Babe in my arms, and to let me fold Him to my heart, that He may be my strength, my courage, and my example.

PRAYER.—Sweet Infant Jesus! I pray Thee come to my help in all my dangers, temptations, and difficulties. Never permit me to forget Thy holy presence.

THE DESERT.

"Who arose, and took the Child and His Mother by night, and retired into Egypt."—St. Matt. ii. 14.

INVOCATION.—My Jesus! I give Thee my heart and my mind.

I. I follow the holy wanderers in spirit as they pursue their flight. Alas, their sufferings are many! The mountain paths of Juda are steep and rugged, winding along the edge of precipices, covered with rolling stones. Joseph and Mary choose the least frequented of these, and consequently the most fatiguing.

II. And now they reach the desert, with its scorching winds, blinding sun, and clouds of sandy dust. They must suffer terribly from heat, fatigue, and thirst! St. Joseph must be footsore. Mary must be sadly weary. And the Child? Must He not suffer, too, lying for so many hours in one position, even although His resting-place is His Mother's arms? His little tender limbs must ache from the pressure of the swaddling-clothes in which they are swathed! But no murmur comes from the lips of those holy three. Mary is grave, and a shade of fear for her Babe crosses her fair brow now and then; but her face breathes calm even as she flies.

III. A little clump of palm-trees and thin-foliaged acacias stand out upon the barren waste of sand. Here is some broken ground, carpeted by a few desert plants and some scanty blades of grass. A crystal spring is bubbling up from under the rocks.

I picture to myself the Holy Family resting in the shade, during the noonday heat. The gentle Mother is seated with Jesus in her lap, her own fatigue forgotten as she ministers to His wants. Angels are around, invisible, adoring. St. Joseph, with tender solicitude, twines the straggling branches of the acacia trees together, the better to shelter the Mother and the Child, draws water from the spring, prepares the frugal meal, and knows no rest until he has done his best for the precious treasure in his charge.

Many are the lessons for me to gather from the journey of the Holy Family. The journeys which I make are surrounded by every comfort, and yet how fretfully do I complain of the smallest inconvenience I may have to bear! Do I not make others suffer, too, from my restlessness and my discontented grumblings at the heat, the dust, or my own hunger and thirst?

RESOLUTION.—Sweet, uncomplaining Babe! I will try to imitate Thee. I will make a firm resolution to bear my little trials silently, for Thy sake. Instead of thinking so much as I do about myself and my own grievances, I will turn my attention to those around me, and, in imitation of St. Joseph, try to alleviate their discomfort.

PRAYER.—Jesus! Mary! Joseph! I pray you give me a contented spirit, and give me grace to compassionate Your sufferings instead of dwelling upon my own.

NIGHT IN THE DESERT.

"Who arose, and took the Child and His Mother by night, and retired into Egypt."—St. Matt. ii. 14.

INVOCATION.—Holy Joseph, by thy love of Jesus and Mary, help me to meditate upon the flight into Egypt, I pray thee.

I. Another long, weary day is drawing to a close. Mary and Joseph have reached the middle of the desert. The slanting rays of the setting sun warn St. Joseph to seek shelter for the night. A few stunted bushes meet his eye. There is no better covering for the Babe! He has no home! Let me think of this, oh! my Jesus, and adore Thee in Thy poverty! It is only the poorest of the poor, the beggars of the streets, who have no homes. The very birds of the air have their nests; the animals of the field have their lairs! Thou alone, the Creator of the world, must lie under the open sky, with a few poor leaves as sole covering for Thy Head!

May the thought of my Saviour, a homeless fugitive, sleeping in the desert, make me thankful to Almighty God for the comforts and blessings which I receive at His hands!

II. The bright, silvery moon comes forth. By its light I fancy I see the sweet Mother spread her veil out upon the hot, yellow sand, and then lay her Babe gently down thereon. He sleeps. His eyelids are closed. The long lashes lie upon the soft cheeks. The little bosom lifts itself in gentle heavings. The breathings are long and regular. I draw near to gaze upon the Infant God. Oh, Mother! teach me to love Him better, this Jesus, Who has become a helpless, persecuted Babe for the love of me!

And now Mary and Joseph fall upon their knees and pray. Their eyes are fixed upon the lovely Slumberer, as we fix our eyes upon the Tabernacle when we pray.

The little Babe lying upon the sand is, indeed, the same God Who dwells in the Blessed Sacrament in our churches, the God Who rules the world, the God of angels; and He is a homeless wanderer upon His own fair earth!

How touching, how beautiful must have been the prayers of Our Blessed Lady and St. Joseph! With what reverence, with what holy devotion they would pray! Their eyes must be heavy with sleep, for they are very weary; but they do not dream of laying themselves down to rest until they have paid their evening tribute of praise and thanks to the

Lord. Here is a lesson for me. Do I never omit my night-prayers? Do I not often hurry them over, considering my fatigue a sufficient excuse for my negligence?

RESOLUTION.—The example of Mary and Joseph shall be my rule. Henceforth I will let no weariness cause me to omit my night-prayers. If serious illness should render me incapable of kneeling before my crucifix—if I am confined to my bed, and my head throbs with pain—I can and will say at least one "Our Father" and one "Hail Mary," thoughtfully and reverently, and so commit myself into God's holy keeping for the coming night.

PRAYER.—Bless me, oh, Holy Babe! Take me into Thy keeping, I pray Thee, and grant me the grace of perseverance in well-doing.

ARRIVAL IN EGYPT.

"... And he was there until the death of Herod."
—St. Matt. ii. 14.

INVOCATION.—My Blessed Mother! grant that I may carry thy Divine Babe in my heart, now, and until my death.

I. The white walls of an Egyptian city rise up out of the green border-land which fringes the desert. A mighty river rolls at their feet. It is the eve of a pagan festival; the streets are full of people. Suddenly a terrific crash is heard. The images of the heathen gods have fallen from their places, and are lying in fragments on the ground! At this moment some travel-worn pilgrims enter the city gate. It is Mary, clasping to her bosom her weary Child, and Joseph. Anxious and perplexed are their countenances. Where shall they find hospitality in this strange city?

The dark eyes of the Egyptians cast wild, fierce looks at the humble strangers. Neither Joseph nor Mary can speak the language of the country. Money they have none. How desolate must they feel!

II. St. Joseph is not known in Heliopolis, and who will employ an untried foreign workman? Who will give credit to strangers, arriving without friends, money, or recommendation? Perhaps—the thought is terrible—they are forced to hold out their hand for alms! Perhaps some kind soul, touched by the sight of Mary's beauty, attracted by the irresistible fascination of the fair Babe in her arms, offers them hospitality for those first few weeks! Whilst Joseph goes in search of work, I can fancy the Blessed Virgin paying her debt of gratitude by rendering humble, kindly services to the Egyptian woman with whom I imagine her to lodge. I fancy the dark-skinned pagan gazing intently on the fair-faced Jewish Mother, wondering whence comes that sweet serenity which fills her poor heathen heart with a strange longing she cannot understand. I fancy this woman growing gentler and kinder day by day; for who could dwell with Jesus and Mary and not grow better?

III. My heart melts with pity as I contemplate Jesus, Mary, and Joseph in their lowly exile! I could weep as I think of their poverty, their humiliations! They must feel so forlorn in this idolatrous land. The common necessaries of life are wanting, and they do not complain. Hard work and obscurity are their lot. They are unknown, unwelcomed, unloved. Jesus would have it so.

His love of poverty makes me feel deeply ashamed of my dislike to anything which resembles humiliation. If the Mother of God is forced to earn her daily bread, I perceive that work is an obligation upon everyone, no matter whether of rich or poor degree.

How often have I not secretly thought needlework—plain-sewing especially—a degrading occupation; that with my abilities I should be better employed in intellectual studies! Here, then, is a rebuke for my foolish pride!

Or perhaps my work is coarse, my fingers ache, my task seems endless. Other children are at play in the sunshine, and I am stitching in a small, close room. The thought of my Divine Mother at her daily toil gives me fresh courage. The Infant Jesus sees me, and smiles upon me. I am consoled and refreshed!

RESOLUTION.—When my heart grows faint, or I am inclined to murmur at my tasks, I will ask Mary to come to my aid, and place myself in spirit at her side.

PRAYER.—Sweet Jesus! I offer Thee all the little sufferings of my daily life, and beseech Thee to make me patient and uncomplaining as Thyself.

SOJOURN IN EGYPT.

"That it might be fulfilled which the Lord spoke by the prophet, saying: Out of Egypt have I called my Son."—St. Matt. ii. 15.

INVOCATION.—Sweet Infant Jesus, grant me to love meekness, poverty, and simplicity of life for Thy sake, I entreat Thee.

I. Years have passed rapidly away. In a quiet, narrow street of the Egyptian city is Joseph's humble dwelling. The door of his workshop is open. Mary is spinning in the entrance, pausing in her work now and again to gaze upon the Child, now no longer a Babe. Poor as is the little house in an Egyptian back street, it is worthy of deepest veneration. How many holy scenes have its walls witnessed! Here Jesus began to walk! Here He spoke His first words! Here Mary made His first tunic, that seamless tunic, which, tradition tells us, grew with Him as He grew. Here Mary took off His swaddling-clothes and gave freedom to His tender limbs! Oh! my sweet Lord, I adore Thy first tottering steps! I adore those first words which tremble on Thy lips! I adore those first lowly offices which Thou dost render Thy Mother and Thy foster-father in the touching weakness of childhood!

II. The little house is a very sanctuary of work. Joseph and Mary must toil hard and late for their daily bread. The distaff or the needle is constantly in the Blessed Virgin's hands, as she employs the arts which she learnt in her girlhood in the Temple, wherewith to share the burthen of St. Joseph's labours. Neither is her house neglected. I watch her as she goes the round of her simple duties, holding the Child on one arm, as with the other she arranges and disposes everything in a beautiful fitness and order which convey a practical lesson to me.

It would be quite impossible to imagine Our Blessed Lady with a fold of her veil or a tress of her hair otherwise than in perfect order. Her every action is done with perfect regularity and at its proper time. The beauty and order of her holy soul are reflected in her exterior, in her words, and in her deeds.

Can I turn to myself, and not blush for shame, when I compare my disorder with Mary's order? Is not disorderliness one of my principal faults? Do I not frequently, alas! idle away my time, putting off doing one plain duty until the time for doing a second arrives, and then fulfilling both hurriedly, in a slovenly, imperfect manner? Do I not often show impatience when I am reproved for any untidiness? Have I never caused serious inconvenience to others by my dawdling, unpunctual ways? Here is matter for reflection and amendment.

RESOLUTION.—I will begin the day by rising promptly when called, and I will then go to all my actions with a firm determination of doing each one at its appointed time.

PRAYER.—Divine Child! grant that my greatest happiness may consist in serving Thee promptly and thoroughly. Mother Mary, teach me by thy holy example to love and practise order, I beg of thee.

RETURN TO PALESTINE.

"But when Herod was dead, behold an Angel of the Lord appeared in sleep to Joseph in Egypt, saying: Arise, and take the Child and His Mother, and go into the land of Israel. For they are dead that sought the life of the Child."—St. Matt. ii. 19, 20.

INVOCATION.—Adorable Jesus! Grant that I may follow thee whithersoever thou goest.

I. Herod being dead, an Angel appeared again to St. Joseph in his sleep, and bade him return to Palestine. St. Joseph obeys at once. The preparations for departure are soon made. There are a few kindly souls to whom farewell has to be said, a few carpenter's tools to be gathered together, a scanty wardrobe to be made into a bundle: that is all. The poor have few worldly possessions.

I watch the Holy Family as they pass through the gates of the city, Joseph and Mary each holding a hand of the Child Jesus. A look of gladness is on the faces of the three. But the desert lies before them, and they have many a long mile to traverse, many a weary step to take.

II. The belt of green vegetation bathed by the waters of the Nile is passed. The holy wanderers are in the great sandy waste once more. This time Jesus is no longer a Babe pillowed in His Mother's arms. He is a fair, gracious Boy, too big to be carried long by Mary or Joseph, too little to walk without much fatigue. The halts of the Holy Family must be more frequent, their weariness even greater than on the former journey. Mary and Joseph must suffer keenly at the thought of the Child's sufferings! Joseph is older, too; his bundle, light as it is, weighs more heavily upon his shoulders. I can imagine the Holy Child, with His feet blistered by the scorching sand, His cheeks fevered by the parching thirst which is one of the torments of the desert, looking up in His anxious Mother's face with a reassuring smile, and perhaps keeping pace with her by a kind of running walk which is pain to His poor little throbbing feet, in order that she may not know His weariness. Mary and Joseph gaze into the depths of those sweet boyish eyes, and their souls are refreshed. The clear tones of that young voice ring like sweet-sounding bells in their hearts, causing them to forget all suffering in the ecstasy of their love.

How touching is this journey of the Holy Child! Surely, dear Lord, Thou hast suffering enough in store for Thee! Why wilt Thou inflict such penance on Thy tender frame?

From the example of the Child Jesus travelling across the desert, I learn to make light of my little aches and pains, when I see that they give anxiety to others.

RESOLUTION.— Instead of murmuring and complaining when I am ill, finding fault with everything which is done for me, constantly desiring something which I may not have, and wearing a peevish look on my face, I will try to lighten the anxiety of those who are nursing me by my cheerfulness, thanking them from time to time for their kindness to me, and accepting my sufferings as penance for my faults.

PRAYER.—My Blessed Lord! grant that I may rejoice instead of complaining when I have some little pain to bear, in union with the fatigue Thou didst suffer on Thy return from Egypt.

NAZARETH.

"He dwelt in a city called Nazareth."—St. Matt. ii. 23.

INVOCATION.—My Blessed Jesus! I offer Thee my heart. Show me Thy ways, I beseech Thee, and teach me to follow in Thy steps.

I. The long line of Juda's hills is visible at last on the horizon. The journey is well nigh over. The holy wanderers have almost reached Jerusalem, when again St. Joseph receives a Divine warning. Herod is dead, but his cruel son reigns in his stead; the Child's life would be in peril at Jerusalem. Tranquilly, calmly, Mary and Joseph turn aside and direct their tired steps on towards Nazareth. Rest seemed within their grasp, and home, under the shadow of that glorious Temple, so dear to Mary's heart. But Joseph and Mary know no will but God's, and the holy calm of their souls can never be disturbed.

From their meek submission to the orderings of Providence, I learn to bear my disappointments unmurmuringly. How often have I not looked forward to some long-promised pleasure, and at the last moment, an unlooked-for circumstance has deprived me of its enjoyment! Do I bear such disappointments patiently? or do I receive them with an outburst of petulant ill-humour?

II. The years roll on and one resembles another to the Holy Family, each being spent in extreme poverty, hard work, and sweet holy intercourse with Jesus. As I draw near in spirit and gaze into the familiar workshop, a touching picture presents itself to my eyes. "Joseph is showing Jesus how to do some work, and his broad man's hand is laid on the small hand of the Boy, and he is gently guiding His fingers. He is doing it mechanically, for he is gazing rather on the Saviour's face than on the work."* Holy Child, I adore Thee in Thy humility, seeming to learn, helping Thy foster-father as far as Thy strength will permit.

Again, III. Pictures rise before my mind of the sweet thoughtful Boy sharing His Mother's household tasks; fetching water from the village well, climbing the steep, grassy path, and pausing to take breath; placing the large earthenware pitcher on the ground, and bending down to pluck a few of the bright-coloured anemones, or delicate-tinted cyclamen which blossom at His feet; gathering wood for Mary's fire, His young shoulders bowed be-

* Faber, "Bethlehem," p. 355.

neath its weight! With what tender, filial love Thou dost Thy actions, my sweetest Lord! How perfect a Son Thou art! How bright is Thy smile as Thou greetest Thy mother!

RESOLUTION.—I will learn from the example of the Child Jesus to be eager in serving and assisting others, and never think any service humiliating or degrading which charity requires of me, after witnessing my God fulfilling the humble tasks of a poor workman's child.

PRAYER.—Sweet Child, receive me into Thy service, I pray Thee, and as Thou didst spend Thy youth in working for the love of me, grant that my whole life may be passed in fulfilling faithfully the duties of my state of life for the love of Thee.

THE HOLY FAMILY GO UP TO JERUSALEM.

" And His parents went every year to Jerusalem, at the solemn day of the Pasch. And when He was twelve years old, they going up to Jerusalem according to the custom of the Feast. . . ."—St. Luke ii. 41, 42.

INVOCATION.—My Blessed Lord, grant that I may know Thee better in order to love Thee more.

I. The law obliged the Jewish people to go up to Jerusalem once a year to celebrate the Pasch. The pious pilgrims travelled by companies, sometimes in detached groups, at others in a long caravan, the men in one band, the women in another. I follow Jesus, Mary and Joseph, watching them by turns, as they sanctify the journey by their holy example and devout conversation.

Jesus is now twelve years old. I picture Him to myself going from one group to another; now offering His Mother those many little attentions which love suggests, now supporting St. Joseph, who is aged and feeble, over a rough piece of ground, carrying brightness with Him to all hearts. I can fancy that all must love Mary's Son. He is a silent Boy, but there is a sweetness in His face and an attraction in His presence which draw all hearts towards Him. "The rough manners of the Nazarenes soften when the sunbeam of His smile is on them. Cold hearts warm, and hard hearts grow gentle, and anger dies away, and all are divinely unmanned as He comes amongst them." ("Bethlehem," by Father Faber, p. 386.)

II. I can fancy the little children gathering round Him, following the gentle, grave-eyed Boy, Who is so ready to listen to their little tales of joy or grief, so sympathizing and loving towards all. I can fancy that the very birds must have sung more sweetly as He passed, and the flowers given out more fragrance as the hem of His tunic brushed their gay petals. Oh, Jesus! grant that I may think of Thy sweet childhood when I am tempted to be unamiable towards my companions or schoolfellows, wrapping myself up coldly in my own little interests, instead of giving them the kindly sympathy they seek from me, and may join in their pleasures and take part in their troubles as though they were my own.

III. I follow Jesus, Mary and Joseph into the Temple. The Child kneels in prayer. Crowds of worshippers are around Him. He heeds them not. His heart is fixed on His heavenly Father. He is offering Himself in sacrifice for mankind. Calvary lies before His mind. He is longing to shed His blood, to die for me!

Jesus was "heard for His reverence," Scripture tells us. Shall I be heard for my reverence? Is my attitude always devout, always respectful? Am I careful to kneel at the proper times during Holy Mass and Benediction? Or do I lounge about, under pretext that I cannot kneel long, thus giving disedification to others by my unbecoming, careless demeanour? When I enter a church, do I take Holy Water devoutly, or as a mere matter of routine? Have I never felt annoyed when my mother, or some one beside me, kneels for a considerable length of time, wondering what she can have to pray about for so long, and testifying my impatience by yawning, fidgeting, noisily turning over the leaves of my book?

RESOLUTION.—I will not allow myself to be so easily distracted in church, but will remember that Angels are worshipping round me on every side, and that if I give an example of bad behaviour, other persons less well-taught than myself may follow it, and that then their faults will lie at my door as well as my own.

PRAYER.—Holy Child Jesus! Increase my devotion, I pray Thee. Grant that I may always remember Thy blessed presence.

LOSS OF JESUS.

"And thinking that He was in the company, they came a day's journey, and sought Him among their kinsfolks and acquaintance. And not finding Him, they returned into Jerusalem, seeking Him."—St. Luke ii. 44, 45.

INVOCATION.—Holy Child Jesus! Enlighten my understanding, I pray Thee. Teach me to love Thee with my whole heart.

I. The pilgrims are gathering together for departure at one of the gates of Jerusalem. The men divide as before into one band, the women into another. As the shades of evening are falling, they meet when the caravan halts for the night. The Boy has not been with His Mother. She, believing Him to be with Joseph, was content, glad in her meek unselfishness that Joseph should enjoy the happiness of His bright presence, although the light goes out of Mary's heart when Jesus is absent from her side.

But what is this? Joseph approaches, and he is alone! Where is Jesus? A vague uneasiness creeps over the Mother's heart. Uneasiness deepens into alarm and anguish as Mary and Joseph seek Him amongst friends and kinsfolk in vain.

II. I picture to myself the sorrowing Mother

passing swiftly from one group to another, with the tears welling up to her eyes as she asks the oft-repeated question, have they seen her Son?

III. In the darkness and alone, Mary and Joseph retrace their steps to the Holy City. Mary gazes into the face of every passer-by. Have they seen her Boy? Some give her a rough answer; others wonder she did not take better care of her Child.

And so Jerusalem is reached. There is not a street which the bereaved pair leave unsearched, not a chance left untried. A gleam of light is kindled in their hearts by the description of a lovely fair-haired Boy to whom a woman had given alms in the street. Another tells of a beautiful little Lad whom she found lying on her door-step when she opened her shutters at break of day. Again another has caught a glimpse, as in a heavenly vision, of a fair Boy bending over the pallet of a suffering child in a poor deserted hovel. Vague as are these tidings, they give balm to the sorrowing Mother's heart. It must have been Jesus, no other boy could be so beautiful! Oh, Mother! thy heart is sad and sore! Holy Joseph, thine eyes are sunken with fatigue and affliction! The grief depicted in your face should inspire sympathy in all beholders. But no! cold indifference, or unjust reproach, is added to your pain. And how meekly, how patiently you bear the thoughtless words!

RESOLUTION.—If I am unjustly blamed, or if cold unfeeling speeches are made me when I am in trouble, and longing for kindness and affection, I will think of the humility of Mary and Joseph, and ask Jesus to give me grace to bear these trials meekly and silently for His dear sake.

PRAYER.—Sweet Mother! obtain for me the grace of perseverance, I entreat Thee. Grant that I may never weary of seeking Jesus.

FINDING OF JESUS.

"And it came to pass, that after three days they found Him in the Temple sitting in the midst of the doctors, hearing them and asking them questions."—St. Luke ii. 46.

INVOCATION.—Holy Mother of God! teach me, I pray thee, to understand the life of thy Blessed Son.

I. I follow Mary and Joseph as they sadly ascend the steps of the Temple to lay their sorrows before the Lord. Close to the gate by which they enter is the Hall of the Doctors, where the wisest men of Israel meet together to interpret the law. The door is half open. Mary's ear has caught a well-known sound. It is the voice of Jesus!

For a moment the Mother and foster-father pause, spellbound. The Boy is standing in the midst of the venerable sages. The youthful figure, with its pure boyish face, so calm, grave, and earnest, stands out in relief against the wrinkled countenances and white hairs of His aged listeners. These are gathered around Him, surprised and awed by the strange authority with which He speaks, asking questions, and appearing to learn, in order that He may teach eternal truths. O Jesus, let me, too, learn in Thy Divine school! Thou art the

Book whence generations of Saints have drawn all science. By listening to Thee they have learnt all wisdom; in looking upon Thee, they have found all virtues; in imitating Thee, they have practised all holiness.

II. And now Mary goes forward. "Son," she says, "why hast Thou done so to us? Behold, Thy father and I have sought Thee sorrowing." Mary has no need to tell her Boy how she has sorrowed. The pale, tear-stained face, and the trembling flush of joy which almost overpowers her, tell their own tale. And yet Jesus answers in mysterious words, "How is it that you sought Me? Did you not know that I must be about My Father's business?"

Mary and Joseph do not understand the hidden meaning of these words, but they know that the Holy Child is God as well as Man. They know that, as time advances, their Boy must fulfil His heavenly mission; and they are content.

There is a lesson for me to learn here. I cannot always, in my inexperience, see the wisdom of such and such a decision taken concerning myself. My elders tell me I shall understand the motives of their conduct when I am no longer a child. I scarcely believe this to be possible, so hard does it seem to resign myself to the present, so confident am I in my own sagacity. At such times as these I will think of the Mother of God, and how meekly she submitted her will and her understanding to the dispositions of Providence which she did not comprehend.

RESOLUTION.— I will refrain from seeking to inquire into the motives of my superiors, and from teazing them with indiscreet questions. I will have confidence in their love for me, and accept their decisions unmurmuringly. I will also be careful not to judge others by their actions, when the motives of those actions are hidden from me; as, could I see the spirit which prompts them, many things which now appear blameworthy would prove to be, on the contrary, highly meritorious.

PRAYER.—Holy Mary! grant that, in imitation of thee, I may keep the words of Jesus treasured in my heart.

LIFE AT NAZARETH.

"And He went down with them, and came to Nazareth : and was subject to them."—St. Luke ii. 51.

INVOCATION.—Sweet Jesus, subject to Thy parents, teach me the beauty of Thy hidden life, I pray Thee.

I. The interior of the Holy House is again before me. Many seasons have come and gone. Spring has followed winter, and summer spring, in many a year, without bringing much change to its Holy inmates. Jesus alone has changed. The tones of His voice are deeper. His limbs are longer, broader, stronger. He is fast growing up to manhood. St. Joseph is failing fast, and Jesus is beginning to take his place at the carpenter's bench, in order to relieve His foster-father and help to support the Holy Family. Never was there so thoughtful, so obedient a Son!

II. I watch Him in spirit, as, with eager tenderness, He lifts the heavy blocks of wood which are beyond St. Joseph's strength, sweetening the daily toil with holy converse. I watch Him as He carries home the work, when finished, to His humble employers, meekly receiving the modest salary of His labour. I gaze upon Him as He seats Himself with simplicity at Mary's frugal board. I follow Him as He wanders out into the fields or vineyards, at set of sun, seeking some sheltered nook where He may pray to His heavenly Father, unseen by men. I adore Him as He kneels upon the ground, His hands clasped, His eyes upturned towards the blue vault above, which my fancy pictures starred with Angels worshipping their Lord.

III. I picture Him returning to the little house, where Mary stands at the doorway waiting for her Son, coming to her side with a gentle caress and kneeling at her feet, asking for His Mother's blessing before He lays Himself down on His hard straw pallet for the night.

O Jesus, I pray Thee, by Thy meek submission to Thy Mother and foster-father, by Thy eager promptitude to do their bidding, by Thy thoughtful care of them, make me tender and obedient to my parents. Grant that I may never wound their hearts by a hasty or disrespectful word. Grant that I may be attentive to their commands, and eager to prove my love for them by my anxiety to anticipate their every wish.

When my father and mother are ill, in any affliction, do I tend them as Jesus tended the aged Joseph? Do I find it a happiness and a pleasure to be near them, or do I feel the confinement of a sick-room, or the presence of sorrow, irksome, showing by my face that I long to be elsewhere? Am I careful to lower my voice, tread lightly, and watch the dear faces, so that I may discern their least requirements?

RESOLUTION.—In memory of St. Joseph, I will show great respect and deference towards all aged persons, and feel it an honour when I have an opportunity of waiting upon them and of rendering them any little service in my power.

PRAYER.—My beloved Jesus! give me a compassionate heart, I beseech Thee, and teach me to imitate Thee in Thy humble life at Nazareth.

JESUS AND MARY.

"And Jesus advanced in wisdom and age, and grace with God and men."—St. Luke ii. 52.

INVOCATION.—My Blessed Lord, fill my heart with Thy love, I beseech Thee, and give me holy thoughts and desires.

I. Jesus and Mary are alone. The sweet soul of Joseph has gone forth to the place of rest where he awaits the resurrection of the Jesus whom he has loved so fondly and tended so faithfully. How peaceful, how beautiful must have been the death of this "just man," in the arms of Jesus and Mary! Dear St. Joseph! Thou wast the saint who wert nearest to Jesus on earth. He can refuse thee nothing. Be thou my special patron, I beseech thee, and help me to live so that I may die in the arms of Jesus.

II. Jesus is now the sole support of His Mother. From early morn till dusk the King of Heaven stands before a carpenter's bench, hewing, sawing, and planing!

A pious tradition tells me that the workshop stood at the distance of a few yards from the Holy House; that near it was a stone-seat, shaded by the spreading branches of a sycamore-tree. Here many a weary, dusty traveller would pause and rest, and watch the grave-eyed young Workman bending over His lowly tasks, and sparing neither pains nor exertion in order to execute them with precision, and would go on his way cheered and refreshed by the sweet atmosphere of peace and holiness into which he had cast a glance.

III. Oh! my Blessed Jesus, grant that I, too, may draw near Thee and learn the lessons Thou wouldst teach me by Thy rude, humble toil! These eighteen years spent in daily hardship and labour tell me that all creatures are bound to labour, as their Divine Model laboured thus. My lot in life may not require manual exertions. I may not be forced to earn my bread. But during my youth, wherever and however it may be passed, knowledge has to be acquired, and this cannot be done without patient, persevering toil. The example of the Divine Artisan will henceforth give me renewed zeal when I feel disheartened by the difficulties before me, when learning is tedious, and study an effort. I will remember that Jesus spent nearly the whole of his life in the practice of ordinary, simple virtues, in order to teach me that perfection does not consist in great and wonderful deeds so much as in the quiet, punctual fulfilment of every-day duties, and in the devout persevering spirit which does all things well, be they great or small, for the glory of God alone.

RESOLUTION.—I will, for the future, respect those who toil for their daily bread, speaking to them kindly when occasion offers, and showing them every consideration in my power.

PRAYER.—Oh, Jesus! model of all virtues, grant me, I pray Thee, that I may love the practices of a common, ordinary life.

JESUS LEAVES NAZARETH.

"And Jesus Himself was beginning about the age of thirty years."—St. Luke iii. 23.

INVOCATION.—Oh, Mother! who didst love thy Son with the purest love, help me to spend my whole life in the study and imitation of Him.

I. A day comes when Jesus, now thirty years of age, lays down His measuring-line and hangs up His workman's tools against the wall for the last time. I can fancy His gentle Mother's eyes resting upon her Son with a wistful look. She knows that the happy, peaceful life in the humble little home at Nazareth is at its close, that Jesus must leave her to go forth into the world to fulfil His divine mission, and manifest Himself to men.

Thou hast long known this, my Mother, but oh, how sad must be thy heart! In all these years of holy intimacy with Jesus He has often spoken to thee of this hour, and behind it—all too near—thou seest rise the shadow of the Cross! But thou art patient and resigned as ever. Never dost thou offer a word of opposition to the will of Jesus! Thou dost not use the gentle constraint of a mother's love, and seek to detain thy Son. Thy face is calm and sweet.

II. I picture to myself the Christ humbly kneeling before His Mother, as He was wont to kneel at her feet as a child, asking her farewell blessing. And the Mother blesses her Son, and then kneels herself to implore the benediction of her God.

III. Jesus is gone! The Holy House has lost its sunshine. Never again will it be gladdened by that gracious Presence! As I contemplate the gentle Mother in her sad solitude, solitude which, alas! is the shadow of that terrible separation to follow three short years hence, my heart goes out to her with love and pity. Long does she stand under the shade of the big sycamore, gazing down the path after the retreating form of Jesus. The tears fill her eyes as she thinks of the long, weary journey He is about to make alone, with no loving Mother to minister to His wants, to bathe His feet when they ache with the heat and the dust and the stones which wound their tender flesh as they go forth to carry the message of love to the world! And when she turns and re-enters the little house, how lonely must she feel!

RESOLUTION.—I will learn from the example

of Our Blessed Lady to bear separation from those I love without repining when God's will requires it. If I feel lonely and sad at heart, I will ask Mary to put her arms round me and press me to her heart. In imitation of her perfect resignation, I will try to accept my little trials and crosses patiently, offering them all to Jesus, and beseeching Him to make me docile to His will.

PRAYER.—Mother of consolation, help of the afflicted, I pray thee be my refuge in all my sorrows, now and until the hour of my death.

BAPTISM OF JESUS.

"And it came to pass, in those days Jesus came from Nazareth of Galilee; and was baptized by John in the Jordan."—St. Mark i. 9.

INVOCATION.—My Blessed Lord, I pray Thee render my heart pure, in order that I may contemplate and know Thee.

I. Many miles away from Nazareth, I behold a great multitude of people gathered together on the banks of the river Jordan. A man is standing at the water's edge, teaching and baptizing in the Name of the Lord. He is clothed in a rough garment of camel's hair, with a leathern girdle about his waist. It is John, the son of Elizabeth, the Saint of the desert, whose life has been a life of penance, although he has never known sin, who lives in the caves of the wilderness, and feeds upon locusts and wild honey, and whose holy solitude, tradition tells us, was gladdened by a glimpse of Jesus once, many years gone by, as the Holy Family returned from Egypt into Palestine.

II. Jesus approaches from out of the shadow of the great grey rocks which overhang the river. Humbly mingling with the crowds who are pressing forward to be baptized, the Lord of all Majesty meekly asks His own creature to give Him also baptism, as though He, too, were a sinner!

It is many years since John has seen Jesus, but the tones of that voice, once heard, can never be mistaken. The Baptist is troubled. Looking earnestly at Jesus, he exclaims, "I ought to be baptized by Thee; and comest Thou to me?" Jesus gently insists.

III. In adoring reverence I gaze in spirit upon my Lord, standing so modestly in the river before the Baptist, the crystal drops glistening upon His sacred brow. And as I gaze, the heavens open, shedding a bright radiance over the waters, and the Holy Ghost descends upon Him in the form of a dove, whilst a voice from heaven is heard saying, "This is My beloved Son, in Whom I am well pleased."

IV. I can imagine the rapt amazement of the multitude at this wonderful scene, and the reverent, adoring attitude of John, as the Eternal Father thus proclaims the Divinity of Jesus on the threshold of His public life.

What a deep lesson of humility this baptism of Jesus teaches me! He begins His public life by taking the position of a sinner, and humbling Himself before His own creature, in presence of a multitude.

A slighting word or look is sufficient to disturb my composure. I strain every effort to be well thought of by others. I blush if the lowliness of my birth or position is publicly mentioned. Or else, perhaps, I have put on a cloak of false humility, spoken of myself in a depreciating manner in the hopes of hearing myself contradicted, and thus have flattered my vanity and pride.

RESOLUTION.—I will try to become so truly humble that I shall feel no surprise when I am slighted or passed over. I will correct myself of my bad habit of noticing the defects of others, and turn my attention to their good qualities instead.

PRAYER.—Jesus, meek and humble of heart, make my heart like Thine!

JESUS GOES UP INTO THE WILDERNESS.

"And He was in the desert forty days, and forty nights; and was tempted by Satan, and He was with beasts, and the Angels ministered to Him."—St. Mark i. 13.

INVOCATION. — My Blessed Lord, by Thy temptation in the desert, I pray Thee come to my aid when I am tempted to sin.

I. Immediately after His baptism, Jesus goes up into the wilderness for forty days. I follow Him in spirit. The mountain-side is full of rocky caves, the haunts of wild beasts. It is a gloomy, desolate spot, far from the habitations of men. Here Jesus fasts and prays, sleeping on the bare ground, exposed to cold, wind, and rain.

I adore Thee, oh, my Saviour, doing penance for my sins! Thou hast no sins to expiate, no faults to conquer. It is for me Thou exposest Thy delicate frame to hardship, to teach me the necessity of self-denial as well as of prayer.

II. A touching legend shows me the gracious Saviour seated on a rock, with savage animals lying peacefully at His feet, and little birds singing sweet songs about His head, as they nestle in the folds of His garments. I learn from the sight of Jesus dwelling amongst animals that purity and innocence attract all hearts, and that if I would resemble Jesus, I must live at peace with all, supporting the defects and ill-humour of my fellow-creatures with patience and charity, showing kindness to those who are rough and overbearing, as well as to the meek and gentle. I learn also to be kind to all dumb animals, which are creatures of Jesus, and which He loves—since He dwells amongst them—and I learn never wilfully to hurt them, but to cherish them, as each represents a thought of the Creator, and a gift at His hands.

III. Towards the end of the forty days, when Jesus is weakened by hunger and thirst and penance, the devil comes to tempt Him. Jesus will suffer every trial, every humiliation which He requires me, His child, to endure. Temptations to gluttony, to avarice, to vainglory, are, turn by turn, put before the Saviour. Meekly and sweetly He submits to the devil's unhallowed treatment.

The struggle over, Angels come and minister to their wearied Lord, bringing Him heavenly food. I picture to myself the sweet form of Jesus, attenuated by His long fast, surrounded by a multitude of these bright, joyous spirits, who are praising Him for His victory over Satan, and bringing Him sustenance wherewith to restore His sinking frame.

My Jesus! I see the lesson Thou wouldst teach me. I see that I shall never resist temptation if I do not practise penance. I must not delude myself with the idea that penance is a virtue reserved for grown-up persons or for Saints. It must be practised by all, especially by me, as all have faults to conquer and inclinations to evil to overcome.

RESOLUTION.—I will practise some act of mortification every day. If I cannot always deny myself in food, I can always mortify my tongue by refraining from idle questions, or from talking about myself—a subject generally wearisome to others.

PRAYER.—My Blessed Saviour! accept these my resolutions, I entreat Thee, and help me by Thy grace.

JESUS BEGINS TO CALL HIS DISCIPLES.

"And the two disciples heard Him speak, and they followed Jesus . . . and saw where He abode, and they stayed with Him that day."—St. John i. 37, 39.

INVOCATION.—Most Gracious Lord, call me, I beseech Thee; make me ever faithful to Thee.

I. St. John is still preaching and baptizing on the banks of the Jordan, when Jesus leaves the wilderness. On seeing His retreating form, the Baptist turns towards two of his disciples, exclaiming, "Behold the Lamb of God." His tone and gesture say plainer than words could have said, "Follow Him."

Jesus, hearing the sound of quick footsteps behind Him, turns and sees the two young disciples following Him, evidently anxious to speak with Him, but hesitating how to approach. "What seek you?" the Saviour kindly asks. Timidly comes the answer, "Master, where dwellest Thou?" "Come and see," Jesus graciously replies.

II. I picture to myself Jesus conducting the two young fishermen to the poor dwelling which He has chosen for His temporary abode. Andrew, the elder of the two, is profoundly moved by the sweet presence of

Jesus, and listens in silence to His holy words.
John, who is, as yet, scarcely more than a
youth, cannot take his eyes from the Saviour's
face. He hangs in ecstasy upon His lips, and
his pure heart goes out at once to the Master
Whom he will love so fondly and so faithfully.

For a whole day the two remain with Jesus,
and then Andrew goes in search of his brother
Simon, eager that the latter may share in his
own happiness, and greets him with the glorious
words, " We have found the Messias."

III. I can fancy the impetuosity with which
Simon would throw down his fishing tackle
and follow Andrew back to the presence of
Jesus. He is older than Andrew, and of an
ardent, impulsive nature. From the instant
he beholds the Christ, he loves Him with an
enthusiasm which is imperfect at the first, but
which tears and sorrow will sanctify. Jesus
looks fixedly at the rough fisherman as he
enters, his face aglow with the eager haste he
has made, and says, " Thou shalt be called
Peter "—words of obscure meaning now, but
which, two years later, receive a wondrous explanation. I can fancy the gentle Saviour
showing hospitality to these first-called disciples, sharing His frugal evening meal with
them, serving them with His own sacred

hands, and binding their hearts closer and closer to Him the while!

The choice which Jesus makes of these ignorant fishermen teaches me how little value I ought to set upon the greatness of this world, and how far superior are simplicity and purity of heart to titles and honours, wit or beauty. Am I not, alas! apt to boast of the nobility of my family, of the important social position which my parents hold? Am I not secretly vain of my own personal appearance, and inclined to look down upon others less gifted or less well-dressed than myself? O Jesus, my meek and humble Lord, grant that when such foolish, sinful pride rises in my heart, I may think of Thee, the Friend and Companion of lowly fishermen!

RESOLUTION.—When I am tempted to indulge in vain, conceited thoughts, I will picture to myself my face disfigured by some horrible malady, and remember that at any moment it might please God to take away the beauty and talent of which I am so proud, and to render me an object of aversion to everyone who sees me.

PRAYER.—Jesus, most meek Saviour.! I pray Thee give me the grace to know my own nothingness.

MARRIAGE AT CANA.

"And the third day there was a marriage in Cana of Galilee : and the Mother of Jesus was there. And Jesus also was invited, and His disciples, to the marriage."—St. John ii. 1, 2.

INVOCATION.—My God, permit me to kneel at Thy feet and to learn the holy lessons Thou dost teach.

I. Jesus and Mary are again together. The Mother has rejoined her Son at a village of Galilee, called Cana, situated at a short distance from Nazareth, at the foot of a range of mountains in a cool, fertile valley. Who can imagine the transports of holy joy with which Mary would welcome her Son, and kneel at His feet in adoration of His sanctity !

A marriage ceremony is taking place. The bride and bridegroom are friends, perhaps relations, of the Blessed Virgin. Whilst the marriage party is at the synagogue, I picture the Mother of Jesus, in her sweet lowliness, actively employed in making arrangements for the coming feast. Presently sounds of music and merriment fill the air, and from out of the thick grove of fig-trees and pomegranates comes a gay procession. Amid clashing of cymbals and dancing, and the waving of green boughs and the scattering of the leaves of flowers, the bridal-party return to the house. I follow them in spirit as they take their places at the festive board. Jesus is there, sympathizing with the joys of His friends, in like manner as He shares in their sorrows, and gladdening the innocent festivity with the blessing of His gentle presence.

II. These Jewish weddings lasted for seven days, and were very numerously attended. The friends of Jesus are poor, and, before the end of the feast, the supply of wine is exhausted. Great is the consternation of the young couple! The watchful eye of the Mother of Jesus notices their embarrassment. Her heart is full of compassion for the troubles of others, be they great or small. Anxious to spare them the humiliation of making known their poverty, she goes up to her Son and whispers in His ear, "They have no more wine." She does not ask Him to remedy the accident. She simply lays it before Him, confident in His power to help. Jesus answers that His time has not yet come, as though He would say that the circumstance is not important enough for the working of His first miracle.

III. But Mary has faith in her Son's tender heart. Without another word she leaves His side and bids the servants do the bidding of Jesus. Mary has not trusted in vain! Jesus can refuse nothing to the pleading of His Mother. He will put the crown upon the hidden love of years by a public testimony of filial respect to that sweet Mother. Six large water-jars are standing behind the guests. These Jesus orders to be filled with water, and then to be drawn and handed to the master of the feast. I can imagine the amazement of the newly married couple, their joy, their gratitude, when they perceive that the water has been changed into delicious wine!

RESOLUTION.—I will ask Jesus and Mary to bless all festivities at which I assist. I will place my eyes, my ears, and my lips in my Blessed Mother's keeping, in order that I may not be carried away by pleasure or excitement, and say or do anything which might be displeasing to Jesus.

PRAYER.—O Jesus, Mary, I pray You bless and sanctify my life!

LAKE OF GENNESARETH.

"He came and dwelt in Capharnaum on the sea-coast, in the borders of Zabulon and of Nephthalim."
—St. Matt. iv. 13.

INVOCATION.—My sweet Lord, receive me into the number of Thy chosen, I beseech Thee.

I. After the marriage-feast the young Galileans, with whom Jesus had spoken, returned to their boats and their nets, little dreaming of the future which was in store for them. Jesus and His Mother go down to Capharnaum, a town on the borders of the lake of Gennesareth which now becomes the centre whence Jesus will make His journeys to and fro. I will draw near and contemplate the lovely landscape, whose very name echoes with the words of Jesus, where the air teems with His miracles and is full of His sweet presence.

Framed by a range of dusky mountains here and there tipped with snow, I behold the azure lake. The softly undulating banks are dotted thickly with towns and villages, whose white roofs gleam in the sunshine through the fragrant groves of orange, mulberry, pomegranate and oleander. Hundreds of sails give life to the glistening sheet of water.

II. Not far from the shore I notice the brothers Simon and Andrew, who are washing their nets. A little farther on is another boat, in which is seated the pure-faced John, mending nets with his father Zebedee and James his brother.

Jesus is walking along the shore. On nearing the boats, He pauses and says to the brothers Simon and Andrew: "Come ye after Me, and I will make you fishers of men." And they, immediately leaving their nets, followed Him. Going on a few steps farther, He comes to the other boat and calls James and John in a similar manner. "And they forthwith left their nets and father, and followed Him."

With what joy must these young fishers have beheld Jesus coming towards them! How powerful must have been the attraction of His sweet countenance! How their hearts must have thrilled at the sound of His voice! I feel inclined to envy these humble friends of Jesus, who became the constant companions of His life. And yet, I have in reality no cause for envy. Faith teaches me that I am as constantly in the blessed company of Jesus as were they. His voice is perpetually sounding in my ear, bidding me follow Him. Do I listen to its soft tones? When the stroke of a clock reminds me that such and such a duty awaits me, do I instantly give up the occupation which I have in hand, and follow Jesus ? When a choice lies before me between indulging my own inclinations or sacrificing them to the wishes of another, do I as unhesitatingly lay down my own desires as the disciples did their nets, because Jesus whispers to me to follow Him ?

RESOLUTION.—I will remember that the voice of Jesus speaks to me from every duty, from every opportunity of practising self-denial, and from every trial or suffering. And I firmly determine never to allow my love of self to make me turn a deaf ear to its holy whisperings.

PRAYER.—Most amiable Jesus ! I offer Thee all my actions, beseeching Thee to perfect them and render them pleasing in Thy sight.

JESUS WORKS MANY MIRACLES.

"And Jesus went about all Galilee, teaching in their synagogues, and preaching the gospel of the kingdom: and healing all manner of sickness and every infirmity, amongst the people."—St. Matt. iv. 23.

INVOCATION.—Divine Jesus! I pray Thee accept the offering I make Thee of my heart and of my mind.

I. The Saviour is dwelling in Simon Peter's house at Capharnaum. Capharnaum is one of those cities near the lake of Gennesareth, whose shaded gardens, carpeted with moss, and studded with bright, gem-like flowers, seem to enjoy a perpetual spring. I picture to myself the Divine Master resting in Simon's house after the labour of teaching the people, healing the sick, and casting out devils for several hours without ceasing. The quiet, peaceful natives of the lake-district are beginning to awaken to the sense of His Divinity, and to follow Him from place to place in vast multitudes.

II. It is early dawn. The sun has not yet risen in the heavens. There is scarcely a glimmer of light to guide the steps of an eager crowd, who besiege the lowly dwelling of the two fishermen, and call vehemently upon

Jesus to come to them. Here are the blind, the lame, the crippled, the palsied, sufferers from loathsome diseases—every form of afflicted humanity. A touching and piteous procession, helped along by the compassionate inhabitants of the town, clamouring for Jesus to come and heal them.

III. But Jesus cannot be found. Simon and Andrew go in search of their Master. They catch a glimpse of His kneeling form at last, half concealed in a grassy hollow of one of the neighbouring hills, whither before daybreak He had betaken Himself for His accustomed prayer. The sweet Saviour upon His knees, in solitude, His Divine countenance a faithful mirror of the holy thoughts which are passing through His mind, teaches me a great lesson—the lesson of combining prayer with work.

I am too apt to allow myself to be absorbed in my occupations. I am, perhaps, employed in some good work which is directly for God's glory—such as decorating His altars, working for the poor, visiting the sick. I throw all my energies into my task, and forget meanwhile that if I am working for God, it is God Who gives me the power to work, and that He has no real need of my puny efforts. I think, perhaps, that whilst I am so busy, I have no time for many prayers, and go so far as to omit my meditation or daily visit to the Blessed Sacrament, forgetting that ten minutes spent upon my knees advance my work more than days of toil unsanctified by union with Jesus.

RESOLUTION.—The example of Jesus praying on the mountain shall remind me never to omit my practices of piety under any pretence whatever. In order to keep my heart in constant union with Him, I will adopt the practice of making short ejaculations of love to Him as often as He gives me grace to remember His sacred presence.

PRAYER.—My God, I give Thee my heart. I desire to love Thee more and more.

CURE OF A LEPER.

"And Simon and they that were with him followed after Him."—St. Mark i. 36.

INVOCATION.—My God, grant that I may hear Thy voice and listen devoutly to Thy teachings.

I. Before Peter has time to reach his Master's side, he is overtaken by the crowd of sufferers. I can imagine the haste with which they follow the disciple, trembling lest they should lose sight of him and so fail to find Jesus.

And now they throw themselves at the Master's feet, surrounding Him, showing Him their infirmities, and imploring Him to cure them, with an importunity which cannot be denied. I picture to myself the figure of the sweet Saviour, just emerging from the sheltered nook in which He has been kneeling, His face still aglow with the Divine ardour of His prayer—the first rays of the rising sun lighting up the bent forms of the motley crowd—the two disciples waiting eagerly to see what new wonders will take place before their eyes. The tender Heart of Jesus is moved by the touching spectacle, and He lays His hands upon the sufferers and cures them.

II. Amongst those who press round the Saviour is a leper, whose terrible and incurable disease has, for years, made him an object of loathing and dread to all. Lepers were forbidden even to approach the habitations of men, for fear of spreading the evil. How has he come hither? A cry of consternation and horror is heard from the crowd as the poor creature timidly approaches and prostrates himself, his face touching the ground, before the Saviour. "Lord, if Thou wilt, Thou canst make me clean," he cries.

Moved with compassion, and touched by the steadfast faith which rings in the voice of the leper, Jesus stretches forth His hand and touches him. A thrill of horror passes through the bystanders at the danger to which Jesus exposes Himself. "I will: be thou clean," the Saviour says; "and immediately the leprosy departed from him."

I can imagine the enthusiasm of the crowd, and the gratitude of the poor leper, who, in his almost overpowering delight at being no longer an object of aversion, hastens to the town, going from door to door, publishing his wonderful cure!

When I see my Divine Lord condescending to touch a leper with His sacred hand, I blush to think of my own squeamishness. Jesus might have cured the leper without touching him, and it seems to me that by doing this, He would teach me the compassion which He would have me feel for the sick poor. I must not think that it is enough to take a remedy to the bedside of a sick person and leave it with a word of inquiry and go my way. The poor are often more grateful for the kind look and the gentle sympathy which asks for particulars of their sufferings, than for the present of food or medicine which is brought them.

RESOLUTION.—When visiting a sick person, I will remember that to turn away from the sight of suffering, wounds or sores, or any object displeasing to my delicacy, may give pain to the feelings of the sufferer. I will, on the contrary, render any little service in my power, such as smoothing the pillows, making the room look neat and cheerful, or reading aloud tender, encouraging words about Jesus.

PRAYER.—My Blessed Lord, by Thy tender compassion give me a love of the poor for Thy sake, I beseech Thee.

THE CALL OF MATTHEW.

"And when He was passing by, He saw Levi the son of Alpheus sitting at the receipt of custom; and He said to him: Follow Me. And rising up he followed Him."—St. Mark ii. 14.

INVOCATION.—My Blessed Lord, I offer Thee all my thoughts. Sanctify them, I beseech Thee, and call me to follow Thee with St. Matthew.

I. A wide road passes through Capharnaum. It extends from Damascus to the shores of the Mediterranean, and is the great highway by which all the rich products of the East are conveyed to the Roman Empire.

Near the town I observe a custom-house, occupied by several tax-gatherers in the Roman employ, a class of men cordially hated on account of their greed and hardness of heart. Indeed, if a Jew entered the service of the customs, he was considered to be excommunicate, cut off from society of the faithful and from all religious privileges.

II. Jesus is walking along by the lake, with a multitude of people following Him. He is probably directing His steps to some sheltered spot on a neighbouring hill-side, where He will teach the people according to His wont. The Saviour's path leads Him past the tax-gatherer's office, where Levi (afterwards St. Matthew) is seated at the receipt of custom. The Master pauses, and looking at Levi: "Follow Me," he says, simply. Without a word, without a question, the tax-gatherer rises, and leaving his employment (a very lucrative one), he follows Jesus.

III. The Scribes and Pharisees, who are ever on the watch to discover an imperfection in the new Prophet Whose growing popularity fills them with a jealous anger, are scandalized and shocked at seeing Jesus admit a tax-gatherer into His intimacy. I can see them scowling upon the humble publican, as the Master graciously enters Matthew's house, and wrapping their long mantles closely round them, as though to avoid contact with a man who eats with publicans and sinners!

Jesus hears their bitter speeches and answers them with the words that He came to save sinners, and to heal those who are sick. What must have been the emotion and happiness of St. Matthew at receiving the Saviour into his house! He is used to hard words, scornful looks and contemptuous avoidance on the part of all Jews; and here is Jesus, the new Prophet Who has risen to teach the people, condescending to sit at his table, speaking to him kindly, and calling him to His intimacy and friendship! No wonder his heart was won on the spot! No wonder he vowed a deep and ardent love to Jesus, and, charmed and fascinated by each word which fell from His lips, treasured up every action of this most amiable Saviour in his heart, to relate them hereafter in his beautiful Gospel narrative!

The example of Jesus teaches me to be kind and gentle towards all, no matter how rough and forbidding their exterior.

RESOLUTION.—When I meet with coldness or unkindness on the part of others whom I have never wronged, I will not judge them hastily, but consider that the hardness of their manner may spring from some hidden suffering. I will be amiable and attentive to them, showing them that I desire their affection, and who knows but that the hearts which seemed so hard may not melt before a few kindly words?

PRAYER.—Jesus, most mild, have pity on me, and help me to imitate Thee.

MIRACULOUS DRAUGHT OF FISHES.

"And it came to pass, that when the multitudes pressed upon Him to hear the word of God, He stood by the lake of Genesareth."—St. Luke v. 1.

INVOCATION.—My God, I pray Thee help me to understand Thy holy lessons.

I. Again the lovely lake is before my eyes. The mid-day heat is on the wane. A refreshing breeze stirs the transparent waters into feathery ripples, whose tiny white crests glitter and dance in the sunlight. Fishermen are mending their nets in the old hulks along the beach. Women are grouped here and there under the shade of the oleanders and of the fig-trees, whose trailing branches reach almost to the water's edge. Little children are playing innocently upon the soft silvery sand.

The Saviour is seated in Simon's boat, and is teaching the people and lifting their hearts from the earthly beauty of the scene to the Creator Who has adorned their fair land with Nature's gifts in such profusion; taking His similes from simple subjects adapted to the minds of His listeners—the lilies of the field, the waving corn, the birds of the air—and conveying the sublimest of lessons to their souls through these familiar images.

Sweet Lord, teach me also, I pray Thee, to find Thee in everything. Grant that the sight of a lovely flower, the sweet notes of a bird, or any of Nature's beauties, may bring Thy love to my mind and lift up my heart to Thee in praise and thankfulness.

II. Closer and closer the people press around the Master. Other fishers catch a glimpse of the Saviour as they return across the lake to the neighbouring towns. The throng at last becomes so great that Jesus, no doubt exhausted by much speaking, bids Simon row farther out upon the little sea, and when they reach deep water, tells him to throw out his net. "Master," answers Peter, "we have laboured all night and have taken nothing." Then, remembering doubtless the miracle of Cana, he adds, "but at Thy word I will let down the net." And lowering the net into the deep, the haul of fish is so great that Peter's net breaks. "And they beckoned to their partners that were in the other ship that they should come and help them. And they came and filled both the ships so that they were almost sinking."

III. At the sight of this miracle, Peter falls on his knees at the feet of Jesus and confesses his unworthiness to remain in the presence of his Lord. I can fancy the astonishment and reverence with which the four fishermen gaze upon the Saviour. Their eyes are opened, and they determine to accompany the Master whithersoever He shall go. "Having brought their ships to land, leaving all things, they follow Him."

What a lesson of confidence this miracle teaches me! Often, like St. Peter, I lose heart when my work is tedious and success does not quickly crown my efforts. I have so little perseverance! In moments of discouragement, I pray Thee, sweet Jesus, come to my help!

RESOLUTION.—Whenever a fresh task is before me, which presents difficulties of accomplishment, I will begin by making an act of humility, confessing my weakness and fickleness of purpose. I will confide less in my own strength and ability, and more in the help of Divine Grace.

PRAYER.—My Gracious Lord, work a miracle in my heart, I pray Thee. Render it humble and give me the grace of a persevering spirit.

JESUS CASTS THE SELLERS OUT OF THE TEMPLE.

" And the Pasch of the Jews was at hand, and Jesus went up to Jerusalem."—St. John ii. 13.

INVOCATION.—My Blessed Lord, I pray Thee increase my reverence as I contemplate Thy Divine actions.

I. Caravans are forming along the shores of Genesareth. The Feast of the Passover draws near. Jesus is going up to Jerusalem, accompanied by His disciples. It is a weary journey of five days, on foot, through the mountain gorges of Samaria; across arid plains, where the sun beats down with vehemence on the travellers' heads.

II. The Saviour enters the Temple for the first time since the public manifestation of His Divinity. Grievous abuses sully the glorious edifice. The vestibule has become a noisy market for the sale of the animals destined for sacrifice. The sacred building itself is invaded, and the bellowing of oxen, the bleating of lambs, the cooing of pigeons, and the chink of money-changers are heard in close proximity to the Holy of Holies, mingled with the noisy bartering of the crowd and the loud disputes inevitable in a public sale.

III. Jesus is determined to purge the Temple of these scandals. Twisting a handful of cords into a scourge, His beautiful face aflame with holy indignation, He drives the animals out of the sacred building, overturns the tables of the money-changers, and bids the sellers of doves " take these things hence, and make not the house of My Father a house of traffic." The majesty of His countenance strikes terror into the hearts of the mercenaries. They do not stay to ask, Who is this who acts with such authority? A scene of wild confusion ensues: merchants hurrying down the steps in pursuit of the flying cattle, usurers hastily gathering up their scattered coin, and the worshippers looking on in mingled awe, surprise and admiration.

IV. I learn from this striking scene the veneration which I ought to entertain for our holy churches, which are not temples of the Holy Spirit only, but contain the living Bodily Presence of Jesus Christ. Here is the Tabernacle which encloses the Blessed Sacrament. Here is the Altar on which Jesus comes down daily to offer Himself as Victim for my sins, and as Food for the souls of men. Here are relics of Saints—telling me of battles fought and won for God's sake. Here are the lamps whose tiny flame is a symbol of Jesus, the Light of the world—the Font, where I was made a child of Christ by the waters of baptism—holy pictures affixed to the walls which touch my heart as they show me the sufferings of my Saviour—a statue of Mary, calling me to the feet of my Mother. I cannot turn to the right or to the left without my eyes resting on some sacred object which calls forth my deepest reverence and love.

RESOLUTION.—Whenever I pass by a church, I will, if possible, enter and say a short prayer. If circumstances do not admit of this, I will bow my head reverently as I pass the dwelling of Our Lord Jesus Christ, and make the sign of the Cross.

PRAYER.—My Blessed Lord! Grant that I may never desecrate Thy Holy House by taking into it a worldly, distracted heart.

MARY MAGDALEN.

"And behold a woman that was in the city, a sinner, when she knew that He sat at meat in the Pharisee's house, brought an alabaster-box of ointment."—St. Luke vii. 37.

INVOCATION.—I give Thee my heart, Divine Jesus. Fill it with Thy love, I beseech Thee.

I. Jesus is at Bethania, a pretty village situated on one of the gentle slopes which surround Jerusalem. He is dining with Simon the Pharisee. The disciples are with Him, and there is a large gathering besides. A large dining-hall rises before my eyes. Round the table couches are placed, on which the guests recline, according to Eastern custom. An open gallery occupies one side of the hall, through the arches of which are seen the distant hills of Galilee in the back-ground; here and there a graceful palm-tree waving its fan-like crest in the balmy breeze, laden with the sweet odours of flowers.

II. Through this gallery, stepping lightly and swiftly, comes a young and lovely woman. The fine silken web of her veil and her embroidered garments speak of riches and luxury. It is Mary Magdalen, the sister of Lazarus, a woman notorious throughout Palestine for her beauty and for her dissipated sinful life. Curiosity had led her one day to listen to

Jesus, as He taught the people. As she listened, and as she gazed at the wonderful Prophet of Whom she had heard so much, a change came over her. She saw her sins in their true light, and an immense desire of reparation filled her heart. If she could only reach Jesus!

III. The lovely face is now pale and tear-stained, as, regardless of the astonished, scornful looks of the assembled Pharisees, Magdalen falls on her knees beside the Saviour. Bending lower and lower, her tears bathe His sacred feet, and then, unrolling the coils of her magnificent hair, she wipes those blessed feet with the long silken tresses. Not a word does she utter, her heart is too full. Taking courage by the Saviour's silence, and the love in her heart welling over, she presses her lips to His feet, covers them with kisses, and pours over them the contents of an alabaster box—the rarest of her perfumes—which fill the guest-room with their fragrance.

IV. Simon now begins to murmur inwardly against Jesus for thus permitting Himself to be touched by a well-known sinner. The Master, reading the uncharitable thoughts of Simon, who cannot see the beautiful mystery of repentance and love in Magdalen's conduct, rebukes him by the blessed words, "Mary's sins are forgiven her, because she has loved much."

The conduct of Simon teaches me not to be ready to think evil of others. Has it not sometimes happened that the behaviour of a person whom I know to be holy has given me a secret feeling of irritation from the sense of my own inferiority ?

From Magdalen's example, I learn that if ever I have the unhappiness to commit a grave fault, I must not delay in seeking forgiveness at the feet of Jesus. The Heart of Jesus is ever kind, ever tender; I have no need to fear. His arms are always open to the repentant sinner !

RESOLUTION.—If my conscience reproaches me with a great fault, I will lose no time in seeking one of God's holy priests and confessing my sin. I may be tempted to say, weakly, to myself, " After all, it is not so long till my regular day for confession." Human respect whispers, "It will be remarked if I go to Confession at an unusual time." That terrible human respect! I will think of the loving Magdalen, braving everything to reach Jesus, and I will not rest until I have bathed his feet with my tears of sorrow.

PRAYER.—Heart of Jesus, most merciful ! Have pity on me and forgive every offence which I have committed against Thee.

THE WOMAN OF SAMARIA.

"There cometh a woman of Samaria to draw water. Jesus saith to her: Give Me to drink."—St. John iv. 7.

INVOCATION.—Help me, I beseech Thee, my Lord, to understand Thy holy teachings.

I. A well is before my eyes in the midst of a lovely valley, enclosed by the mountains of Samaria. The flat roofs and dome-like minarets of a town are visible in the distance, embosomed in a grove of myrtle, oak and olive trees.

Jesus is seated on the low wall which protects the well. He is faint and weary, for He has walked far in the noon-day heat. The disciples have gone forward to the city to buy food. As I gaze upon the Divine Saviour and adore Him in His weariness, I fancy that His eyes are resting upon the mountain which towers in front of the well, and bears upon its summit a temple which the idolatrous Samaritans have built out of hatred to Jerusalem, and that His Heart yearns towards this misguided people.

II. And now I perceive a woman approaching along the narrow path leading over the hill from Sichar. An earthenware jar is upon her head. Her gaudy-coloured costume and striped head-gear bespeak her as a native of Samaria. As she lowers her vessel into the well, Jesus speaks to her. "Give Me to drink," the Saviour says. The woman looks up surprised, for the Jews hold no communication with the Samaritans, and she sees by His dress that Jesus is a Jew. Greater still is her amazement when Jesus goes on to tell her that He is the Christ Who has come to teach and to save all mankind. He tells her, too, many of the secrets of her heart, many of the circumstances of her past and present life, and finally wins her love by the Divine attraction of His sweet presence. Grace works powerfully in her soul. She is eager that all should share in her wonderful happiness, and, putting down her water-jar, she runs at full speed back to the town, telling everyone whom she sees of her having found the Messias, and bidding them seek Him at Jacob's Well.

III. "Give Me to drink!" These words echo in my ear. They bring me in spirit to the foot of another fountain of Grace. I kneel before the Tabernacle of my Lord, where it seems to me that I hear a voice saying unceasingly, "Give Me to drink!" Jesus thirsts for my soul. He thirsts for my love, for my worship! He longs to enter my poor, miserable heart! He calls me by my name—there is no mistaking that Divine Voice! Oh! my Jesus, I come at Thy call. I will not keep Thee waiting longer! Grant that I may have grace to receive Thee oftener and more worthily than heretofore.

RESOLUTION.—The thought of my Saviour's weariness and exhaustion at the well-side shall teach me to have a great veneration for holy priests and religious who endure fatigue, hunger and thirst in their divine pursuit of souls. I will show them all the respect of which I am capable, and esteem it a privilege to contribute in any way, however small, to their temporal necessities.

PRAYER.—Most Gracious Jesus, fill my heart with Thy grace, I beseech Thee. Teach me to love Thee more and more.

THE RULER'S CHILD AND THE CENTURION'S SERVANT.

"Now after two days He departed thence; and went into Galilee."—St. John iv. 43.

INVOCATION.—Speak to my heart, I pray Thee, sweet Lord, and make me obedient to Thy commands.

I. The return of Jesus into Galilee resembles a triumphal procession. The fame of His doings in Jerusalem has stirred the inhabitants to yet greater enthusiasm about their Prophet. Even the heathen Romans hear reports of the miracles worked by Jesus, and a dawning of faith glimmers in their hearts.

On the road between Cana and Capharnaum I behold a Roman official hastening along. His son is dying. He has heard of Jesus. He will seek Him, and entreat Him to cure his son. He finds Jesus at the village of Cana, and beseeches the Saviour to come down quickly and heal his child. Doubtless his faith is hesitating, for Jesus, instead of answering with His usual ready sympathy, replies, "Unless you see signs and wonders, you will not believe." The sorrowing father is not to be rebuffed. His child is dying, and nothing short of a miracle can save him. I can fancy the tears rolling down his cheeks, as he implores the Master to come before the child be dead. "Go thy way," the Saviour gently bids him; "thy son liveth."

II. I picture to myself the poor heathen father hurrying homewards, scarcely daring to hope that the words of Jesus meant that his boy was cured, and the servants meeting him with the glad tidings that the child was still alive. How joyfully must the ruler have clasped his son to his heart! How minutely must he have related every word and gesture of the Saviour to his household! What acts of praise and faith and thanksgiving must have ascended to heaven from this family, who now believe in Christ!

III. As Jesus pursues His way, a vast concourse of people is to be seen coming towards Him from Capharnaum, with the chiefs and elders of the synagogue. The servant of a Roman centurion lies sick unto death. The centurion is an idolater, and fears to approach Jesus; so he has sent a message to Him by personages whom he thinks the Master will not refuse to hear, begging Him to cure the servant whom he loves.

The Master quickens His steps. The centurion, who is watching from a distance, when he sees Jesus coming in the direction of his house, is filled with gratitude, and with a sense of his own unworthiness to receive the Saviour. Taking courage, he throws himself at the feet of Jesus, exclaiming, " Lord, I am not worthy that Thou shouldst enter under my roof: but only say the word, and my servant shall be healed "—a magnificent profession of faith, which excites the admiration of Jesus Himself, Who heals the absent servant on the spot.

In both these miracles the Saviour rewards faith by an exercise of charity. He cures both sufferers; but whereas He is ready to hasten to the bedside of an ordinary soldier's servant, He does not offer to enter the house of the powerful official whose own son lay dying.

RESOLUTION.—When I have an opportunity of practising charity, I will not let myself be influenced by outward appearances. In giving alms, how often have I bestowed my little offering on a person whose face pleased me, and passed over another whose misery was far more pressing! Henceforth I will strive to imitate Jesus by practising humility in all things.

PRAYER.—Most humble Jesus! grant that I may always do Thy will.

THE WIDOW OF NAIM.

"And when He came nigh to the gate of the city, behold a dead man was carried out, the only son of his mother; and she was a widow."—St. Luke vii. 12.

INVOCATION.—Show me the beauty of Thy countenance, sweet Lord, I pray Thee, and teach me to follow in Thy steps.

I. Naim "the Beautiful" is before me, a town situated at the foot of Mount Tabor. Jesus is about to enter the gate of the little city, when a funeral procession emerges, and comes slowly down the road.

I picture to myself the Saviour standing aside, His sacred Head uncovered in presence of the dead, and the crowds of people, who now follow the Master's steps everywhere, testifying respect by their sudden silence, as they fall back in two lines on either side of the road. Slowly and mournfully the procession advances. The hired weepers fill the air with their loud wailings, and almost drown the sound of the musical instruments which are carried next in file.

Now come the friends and relatives of the dead, and finally an open bier, on which rests the corpse, dressed, according to Oriental custom, in the clothes worn during life. The body is that of a youth with a calm, pure face, whom I could fancy a sleeping child, as he lies so peacefully amidst garlands of flowers and soft draperies.

II. Close behind the bier, veiled from head to foot, is the mother, a widow. She is following her only child to the grave. Sobs shake her frame, as she drags herself along, utterly crushed beneath her woe, and followed by the sympathizing inhabitants of the little town. The tender Heart of Jesus cannot look upon such a scene unmoved; perhaps the thought of His own loving Mother crosses His mind. He makes a step towards the afflicted widow, and bids her "Weep not;" and then going forward, He touches the bier. The bearers halt. With a look of majesty indescribable, in tones which thrill through every bystander, Jesus bids the corpse arise!

III. I can fancy the amazement with which the multitude, breathless from excitement, watch the dead youth sit upright on the bier, the colour coming back into his pale 'cheeks, his eyes opened wide with a bewildered, wondering look. He speaks! He lives! I picture to myself the Saviour bending over the boy, lifting him from his flowery bed, and placing him in the arms of his mother. And now cries of admiration and delight burst from the people, and the happy widow, trembling with joy and emotion, throws herself at the feet of Jesus, kissing them again and again!

Oh, Jesus! how tender Thou art! how divinely kind! There is not a sorrow which does not find an echo in Thy Heart!

I look at myself, and what do I behold? Is my heart pitiful and compassionate towards the woes of others? Alas, no! I turn away from the sight of grief. I excuse myself by saying, "What can I do? My words are so cold, so trivial, they could not possibly be of comfort to the sufferers."

RESOLUTION.—I will, with God's grace, conquer my selfish habit of shunning those who are in sorrow. When my sympathy cannot find words in which to express itself—when I know not "what to say," in fact—I will pray to Jesus to touch my heart with a spark of His Divine pity.

PRAYER.—Most compassionate Jesus! I pray Thee soften my heart, and fill it with love of Thee.

KINDNESS OF JESUS.

"Suffer the little children, and forbid them not to come to me."—St. Matt. xix. 14.

INVOCATION.—Most amiable Jesus! I offer Thee my heart. I pray Thee fill it with Thy grace.

I. We have no picture of Jesus in His sacred humanity. All we know of His personal appearance is that He was the most beautiful of all the children of men. Still, who is there who is not aware that, even amongst mortals, the beauty of a soul finds its reflection in beauty of feature? and that purity of heart, innocence of life and interior holiness, transform the plainest countenance and imbue it with a certain winning beauty impossible to describe?

What then must have been the loveliness of the Face of Jesus? What must have been the expression of His eyes, those "windows of the soul," whence shone sweetness, majesty and the tenderest compassion, all combined? Love glowed in every line of His countenance— love of souls, love of sinners, pity for the afflicted, sympathy with all!

Oh! Jesus, I kneel at Thy feet and gaze into Thine adorable countenance. Grant me to look upon Thee until a reflection of Thy Divine beauty may penetrate my poor, cold heart!

II. Little children are special objects of the love of Jesus. They follow Him everywhere, drawn by the sweetness of His face. They come round Him in joyous, fearless troops, sure of a gentle caress, eager for a smile.

Sometimes the patience of the disciples is tried by the pertinacity with which the little creatures cling round the Master and push their way to His side through the densest crowd. They seek to drive the children away, but Jesus will not permit this, and rebukes the disciples, saying, "Suffer the little children, and forbid them not to come to Me."

III. The disciples are one day arguing among themselves about greatness in heaven. Jesus calls one of the little children playing near, and placing him in their midst, tells them that unless they become humble as the little one who stands there, his dark eyes turned inquiringly first on the Saviour, then on the disciples, they shall not enter heaven; and finally He bids them be careful never to "despise one of these little ones."

Here is a lesson for me. I am often sadly

wanting in patience and gentleness with little children. Their noisy prattle disturbs and annoys me. In my ignorant pride I consider myself immeasurably superior to these innocent little beings. Alas! might not the Saviour rebuke me for despising the little ones He loved so much?

As I gaze longer and longer into the sweet face of my Lord, I feel how sadly un-Christlike is my face. My heart is warm perhaps, but out of a sort of false pride, I shut my good feelings tightly therein, and then I wonder that others are not attracted towards me, and that so little affection is shown me!

RESOLUTION.—Henceforth I will ask Jesus to make my heart His dwelling, and then His sweetness will shine through my eyes and upon my lips. I will remember that it is not enough to *feel* kindly disposed, I will show kindness in my face and in my voice, as well as by my words and deeds.

PRAYER.—Sweet Jesus! take my heart, I beseech Thee, and widen it, so that I may love Thee more and more.

JESUS STILLS THE TEMPEST.

"And when they were sailing, He slept; and there came down a storm of wind upon the lake, and they were filled, and were in danger."—St. Luke viii. 23.

INVOCATION.—My Blessed Lord, increase my faith, I beseech Thee.

I. Jesus is teaching on the banks of the lovely blue lake of Genesareth. The sun is sinking low in the heavens, and the Saviour bids the eager crowd of listeners regain their homes whilst it is yet light. Spent with fatigue, He enters a boat, and, bidding His disciples cross over to the other side, He lays Himself down to sleep. My sweet Lord! I adore Thee, as I picture Thee to myself, Thy head pillowed on one arm, Thy beautiful face upturned towards the sky, wearing upon it that peaceful look of close union with God the Father which it never loses, waking or sleeping! From time to time the disciples cast loving glances upon their Master. Not a sound breaks the silence save the sighing of the gentle breeze in the flapping sail, and the rippling of the tiny wavelets against the boat as it glides along.

II. Suddenly a puff of wind is felt. A sound of distant thunder is heard. One of the sudden storms so common in mountainous districts bursts upon the little sea. Thick, murky clouds roll across the sky, the wind rushes in gusts down the neighbouring gullies, lashing the tranquil surface of the waters into angry, foaming waves. The little bark is tossed hither and thither. The helm is powerless. The disciples—fishermen from childhood—are used to rough weather, but they cannot cope with such a storm as this. Seeing that the waves are pouring into the boat, they awaken Jesus with a loud, terrified cry, " Lord, save us, we perish !"

III. The Saviour rises to His feet. His sweet, sonorous voice rings out clear above the tempest's roar. "He commanded the winds and the sea, and there came a great calm." And now Jesus turns to His astonished disciples and tenderly reproaches them, asking them how could they fear when He was at their side ? " Why are ye fearful, O ye of little faith ?" the Saviour says.

I marvel to myself that the disciples should have been affrighted when the Master was with them in their boat; and yet, where is my faith when the waters of trouble or the hurricanes of temptation beat against my heart ? I turn to Jesus, I pray to Him, and He does not seem to hear me. I grow discouraged, faint-hearted. I say to myself, "My prayers are not heard, it is of no use to continue my requests;" forgetting that never for one single moment are the loving eyes of Jesus averted from my soul; and that, if He seems to sleep, it is only because He wishes to be asked more fervently, importuned more perseveringly.

RESOLUTION.—Henceforth, when my prayers are unanswered, when I am inclined to lose heart, I will think of the little tempest-tossed boat, with Jesus sleeping during the storm; and I will take fresh courage from the knowledge that He is at my side, and that, near Him, there is no cause for fear. I will remember too, that if my petitions are not granted, it is, perhaps, because they are displeasing to Jesus; and I will take care, when making a request, to add, "If it be Thy gracious Will;" confident, that if this request be not granted, my loving Lord will send me another unasked grace in its stead.

PRAYER.—Oh! Good Jesus, I pray Thee give me an ardent faith and complete submission to Thy Holy Will.

THE DAUGHTER OF JAIRUS.

"And there cometh one of the rulers of the synagogue named Jairus; and seeing Him falleth down at His feet."—St. Mark v. 22.

INVOCATION.—I beseech Thee, sweetest Lord, send Thy Holy Spirit into my heart, that I may know and love Thee.

I. Scarcely has Jesus set foot on shore when one of the heads of the synagogue, named Jairus, prostrates himself at His feet, beseeching Him to come and heal his little daughter, who lies at the point of death. "And He went with him, and a great multitude followed."

Before the house of Jairus is reached, a messenger meets the afflicted father, and whispers in his ear, "The maiden is dead; why trouble the Master?" Jesus hears the words, and turning an encouraging look on Jairus, bids him, "Fear not: only believe." Jairus follows the Saviour, trembling between grief and a vague hope.

II. As they near the house, sounds of music and wailing greet the ear. Large lamps are already lit in the chamber of death. Hired mourners and minstrels are there, filling the air with lugubrious sounds. The mother of the little girl is seated on the ground, draped in a garment of sackcloth, almost distraught with grief at the loss of her only child.

III. "Why make ye this ado?" asks Jesus, as He stands on the threshold. Then, regardless of the murmurs of the hired wailers, He orders the room to be cleared, permitting none to remain except the father and mother, Peter, James, and John. Going up to the bier on which the dead child is lying, the Saviour takes her cold hand in His, and says to her, "Talitha cumi"—"My little damsel, arise!"

The maiden obeys! Springing from her couch, she begins to walk, wondering, no doubt, why her father and mother gaze at her so strangely! The Master bids the astonished parents give their child to eat, and hastens from the scene, anxious to escape the acclamations of the multitude.

Again I have seen my Saviour work a miracle in response to faith. "Only believe," He says.

What, then, is this virtue, this faith which Jesus desires so ardently to find in our hearts? Faith is the knowledge of Jesus. Faith teaches me all that Jesus has taught, revealed, and enjoined. Faith means Jesus Christ known, loved, and served. The *practice* of Faith means my good actions—acts of piety, meekness, charity, and humility. Am I then *faithful* to my Saviour ? Do I know Him and love Him ?

RESOLUTION.—Henceforth I will endeavour to show by my conduct that I am full of faith. The examples of the Saints—those grand lovers of Jesus—shall teach me how to serve Him. The teachings of Holy Church shall be the lamp to guide my steps. I will venerate the outward signs of my faith, such as Holy Water, blessed candles, my branch of palm, and never allow human respect to cause me to neglect or hide the practices of my religion.

PRAYER.—I pray Thee, sweetest Jesus, make me faithful, even unto death.

CHOICE OF THE APOSTLES.

"And having called His twelve disciples together, He gave them power over unclean spirits, to cast them out, and to heal all manner of diseases, and all manner of infirmities."—St. Matt. x. i.

INVOCATION.—My blessed Lord, I pray Thee fill my heart with respect for Thy Church.

I. The sweet Saviour has passed the entire night in one of His favourite solitudes, not far from the town of Bethsaida. Sleep has not closed His eyelids for one moment, so ardent has been His prayer for the Church which He is on the point of founding. Hitherto, a few only of the Galileans who believe in Him have followed Him from place to place as His friends and companions. Now He will single out twelve from the number of His disciples, to be the foundation-stones of His Church.

II. At dawn of day, Jesus descends into the town, and calling the twelve disciples whom He has chosen, He takes them up with Him to the "desert-place" where He had spent the previous night.

I picture to myself the Saviour, a look of profound recollection on His meek, grave countenance, a little in advance of the disciples, climbing the steep, rocky path which winds up the mountain-side through the olive-groves and vineyards.

I imagine Him seated on a moss-grown stone, the twelve disciples grouping themselves round their Master, wondering wherefore He has called them thus together, and wherefore His beloved Face wears so unusually solemn an expression.

And now the Saviour unfolds their future mission to the Twelve. He institutes them Apostles, giving them power to preach in His Name, to cast out devils, and to heal all manner of diseases.

III. Their names are Simon surnamed Peter, and Andrew, James and John, Philip and Bartholomew, Matthew and Thomas, James the son of Alpheus and Simon Zelotes, Jude the brother of James and Judas Iscariot. Eleven are natives of Galilee, simple, unsophisticated men. One only is a Jew, and he is a traitor. The greater number are fishermen or humble artisans. One has been a tax-gatherer. Truly, it is not on earthly science that Jesus depends for the future glory of His Church!

Jesus speaks. These poor men must be poorer still. Defenceless, they must carry no arms, not even a staff. Ignorant, they must not even think of what they will say; the

Holy Ghost will teach them. Poor servants of a poor Master, they will be despised of men, persecuted, scourged, and put to violent deaths.

In the lives of the Apostles I trace the history of the Church up to the present day —hated of men, persecuted, but always triumphant in the power of Christ.

RESOLUTION.—I am a poor, weak child, incapable of great deeds or great sacrifices. I dare not hope to shed my blood for Jesus Christ. I will give the successors of His Apostles all the help in my power by alms and prayers, and will fix some special sum of money to be subscribed to the " Propagation of the Faith."

PRAYER.—My Blessed Lord, increase my devotion to Holy Church, I entreat Thee.

THE TWELVE APOSTLES.

"And He sent them to preach the kingdom of God."—St. Luke ix. 2.

INVOCATION.—Most Gracious Jesus! grant me to understand Thy sacred teaching, I entreat Thee.

I. I draw nearer and contemplate the chosen twelve. As I gaze, I fancy that a series of pictures is unrolled before my eyes, and the life of each Apostle painted thereon in shining colours, with their symbols, by which all men shall know them.

PETER is first: the ardent, impulsive fisherman I know so well. Rome rises before me. A crucifixion. The Apostle stretched out head downwards. A bunch of keys is his symbol.

ANDREW, a fisherman also. A silent, loving soul. I catch a glimpse of his figure evangelizing many lands, and then joyfully clasping a cross. I see him hanging, bound, not nailed —agonizing until two suns have set. His symbol is a cross, X shaped.

JAMES, SON OF ZEBEDEE, a fisherman. The first to die of all the twelve. His symbol is the sword with which he was beheaded.

JOHN, the beloved disciple. I see a pure-

faced youth leaning on the breast of Jesus.
I see him taking the Mother of God to his
home. I see Rome and a cauldron of boiling
oil. I see a bare, desolate island and an aged
Apostle writing down revelations of Heaven.
His symbol, an eagle.

PHILIP, native of Bethsaida. A contemplative, absorbed in meditation of the Scriptures.
An idolatrous Asiatic city comes before me,
and the martyred Apostle hanging by the
neck from a pillar. A little cross his symbol.

BARTHOLOMEW, the meek Nathaniel. Heathen
lands pass rapidly before me. A martyr crucified head downwards, then flayed alive. Symbol, a knife.

MATTHEW, the humble tax-gatherer. A life
consumed in the study of Jesus and the teaching of the people. Symbol, a man.

THOMAS. I see before me Jesus risen, showing the marks of His glorious wounds. Then
many heathen cities, many conversions. At
last India and a kneeling Saint rapt in prayer,
attacked by a band of armed men with swords
and spears. Symbol, a lance.

JAMES THE LESS. A face bearing a striking
resemblance to that of Jesus. Jerusalem
glitters in the distance. From her towers a
holy martyr is cast to the ground, who prays

on his knees as he is stoned and beaten to death. Symbol, a club.

THADDEUS, or JUDE. Dear to Jesus for his activity and zeal. Symbol, the martyr's palm.

SIMON, a native of Cana. I see the sandy deserts of Egypt and Libya. An island in the West. Multitudes evangelized and the martyrdom of the Apostle. Symbol, a chalice.

JUDAS ISCARIOT, a Jew, native of Karioth. A man with a false face. A garden comes before me. A traitor's kiss, and then a wretched culprit hanging dead from the bough of a tree.

II. The scroll is ended. The picture fades away, and I kneel in turn at the feet of eleven of these glorious Apostles, and beg each of them to give me one of their virtues and a spark of their faith.

RESOLUTION.—I will spend more time in reading the lives of Saints and Martyrs than I have hitherto done, and choose some special point in each life to imitate.

PRAYER.—Holy Apostles of Christ, have pity on me, and teach me to love Jesus with all my heart.

JESUS AND THE APOSTLES.

"And it came to pass afterwards, that He travelled through the cities and towns, preaching and evangelizing the kingdom of God; and the twelve with Him."—St. Luke viii. 1.

INVOCATION.—My Blessed Lord, I follow Thee. Teach me to understand the beauty of Thy life, I beseech Thee.

I. I contemplate the Divine Master in the midst of His chosen family. The hearts of these twelve Apostles are warm, but their ways are often rough. They have but a dim perception of the Divinity of the Saviour. They often trouble Him with indiscreet, inopportune questions. He must suffer from their imperfections, their want of courage, their misplaced zeal, their frequent inability to comprehend His words.

And yet how patient He is with them! How sweetly He condescends to explain His meaning, sometimes over and over again! How gently and delicately He reproves them for their faults!

II. The Saviour's life is as humble and as poor as were the lives of His lowliest followers. It is passed in going from place to place; on foot; under rain and hail, biting winds and burning sun; across rugged mountain-paths and dusty, shadeless plains. Often these journeys lead Him far from the homes of men. Days and nights are spent in fatiguing march, when, for all nourishment, the Creator of heaven and earth contents Himself with a morsel of bread, or a handful of wild fruit gathered on His path, which He eats, meekly seated on the ground, quenching His thirst at the nearest spring.

III. And where does Jesus sleep on these journeys throughout the length and breadth of Palestine? Ah! where, indeed? The Gospels do not tell. It may have been in the hollow of a mountain-side that He took His short rest, or in a rocky cavern by the banks of the Jordan, or it may have been in one of the open inns to be found at the entrance to all towns. More often, I picture the sweet Saviour rising when the tired disciples are asleep, and going into some solitary nook to pray, and if the night be chilly, I fancy Him, as He passes the sleeping forms of the twelve, tenderly covering them over with His sacred hands.

What a world of lessons are conveyed to me by the contemplation of Jesus with His disciples! I blush with shame when I compare my impatience, my conceited self-importance, with His humility and condescension.

I, who am so full of defects, can scarcely tolerate a failing in my neighbour. I expect consideration and deference from my equals, and Jesus bears with the faults and importunities of His creatures with unalterable sweetness! If I am asked to give an explanation twice over, I do so in a tone which implies that my time is too precious to be wasted on such trifles; never reflecting that, by my unwillingness to oblige, I am doing worse than wasting time: I am wanting in charity! I am grieving Jesus!

RESOLUTION.—For the future I will strive to be amiable towards all with whom I live. I will never grudge the time which I spend in assisting others, and will give them my help cheerfully, not allowing them to perceive that they are a trial to my patience.

PRAYER.—Sweet Lord! I pray Thee make me blind to the defects of others, and keen-sighted with regard to my own faults and shortcomings.

THE POND OF BETHSAIDA.

" Now there is at Jerusalem a pond, called Probatica, which in Hebrew is named Bethsaida, having five porches."—St. John v. 2.

INVOCATION.—My Blessed Lord, grant that I may follow Thy steps, and listen to Thy sacred teachings.

I. Jerusalem is before me. The rays of the evening sun are gleaming upon her white roofs and terraces, and illuminating the cupolas of her proud Temple with a golden glory.

At one of the twelve gates of the city there is a spring, whose waters have healing properties. I behold a circular colonnade round the basin, and a flight of steep steps leading down to the water.

This colonnade is filled with suffering creatures. The lame, the blind, the crippled, the diseased, are gathered together in a compact crowd, waiting for the "Angel of the Lord" to descend and stir the waters of the pond. From time to time (once a year, holy authors think), when the pond is agitated, the first person who plunges therein is cured of his infirmity, be that what it may.

II. As I gaze upon this crowd of sufferers, gesticulating and pushing for a position near the steps, I notice a poor, palsied man lying on a mattress. He has been afflicted with his terrible malady for eight-and-thirty years.

Suddenly the sweet, compassionate tones of the Saviour's voice fall upon my ear. Jesus has entered the porch, and is bending over the palsied sufferer, and asking kindly how long he has been thus afflicted. The poor man has never seen Jesus, so that when the Saviour says, " Wilt thou be made whole?" he answers sadly that there is no one who will help him down the steps; that his limbs are paralyzed, and that whilst he is painfully making his way down, others push him aside and get before him.

III. I can fancy the forlorn old man gazing into the Saviour's face as he speaks, and thinking how sweet a face it is! I can imagine his amazement when the stranger, in a voice of gentle authority, bids him take up his bed and walk! The palsy has left him! His limbs are supple and strong as in the days of his youth! "Who is this Who has wrought this miracle?" I can hear him asking, as he lifts his bed from the ground and looks for Jesus. But Jesus has disappeared.

Of all these sufferers, there is only one

whom Jesus heals, and He has pity on this one because of his thirty-eight years' patient perseverance! How often do I pray to Jesus that He will cure me of my besetting sin, and years pass, and I am still not cured! Why is this? Because I have not really *desired* my cure. I have asked for it in a half-hearted spirit, secretly dreading the efforts I should have to make in order to conquer my bad habits.

RESOLUTION.—I will never be discouraged, no matter how many are my faults, or how difficult to cure. I know that the grace of Jesus is waiting for me, not once a year, but always.

PRAYER.—Sweet Lord, I offer Thee all the sacrifices of my own will which I may be called upon to make, and beseech Thee to give me the virtue of perseverance.

JESUS IS FOLLOWED BY A MULTITUDE.

" And a great multitude followed Him, because they saw the miracles which He did on them that were diseased."—St. John vi. 2.

INVOCATION.—My Blessed Lord, I pray Thee give me the grace of recollection and devout attention.

I. The eastern side of the lake of Gennesareth is before me. I behold a long, undulating chain of hills, their flat summits covered with verdure. A few shepherds' huts are dotted here and there, and the green slopes are speckled with browsing flocks. Now and again the musical tinkle of a sheep-bell vibrates on the air, or the voices of the fishermen, who are hanging out their nets to dry in the little hamlets clustered at the feet of the hills, on the shores of the inland sea. Otherwise a peaceful stillness reigns.

II. A boat is sailing swiftly across the lake. It is the bearer of Jesus, Who, with His disciples, is on His way to these solitary plateaux. His enemies are numerous now, and the Jews are already seeking how they may put Him to death. The Saviour and the Apostles are weary; Jesus has been teaching and healing throughout the day, "and they had not so much as time to eat;" and therefore the Master had said to the Twelve, "Come apart into a desert-place and rest a little."

III. Not long, however, is Jesus permitted to enjoy repose. Some one on the beach at Capharnaum saw the departure. The course of the little vessel is watched. The news flies from mouth to mouth of the direction which the Master is taking; the multitudes who know Jesus follow Him, making the circuit of the lake on foot. The inhabitants of the villages and towns through which they pass swell their numbers. By some means the news spreads to the opposite shore; and from the country on the other side of the eastern hills the people come flocking in, band after band, until the number of persons amounts to over five thousand, without counting the women and the children.

Jesus is touched by the devotion of the people. Weary as He is, He cannot refuse to teach them when they have travelled so far.

IV. I behold the Saviour in spirit leaning against one of the low, bushy trees which grow at the top of the hills, and the vast crowds spreading themselves out around Him over the gentle undulations—silent and absorbed, scarce daring to move, lest they should lose one syllable of the precious words which are ringing with silvery sweetness through the air.

I learn from the ardour with which these crowds seek the Saviour how eagerly I, too, must seek Him. I am too apt to leave my acts of devotion for church only. It is true that it is easier to find Jesus in His Tabernacle than anywhere else; nevertheless, I know that there is not a good action, a holy resolution, a duty faithfully performed, in which He is not hidden, waiting for me to come and find Him there!

RESOLUTION.—Like the multitudes of Galilee, I will listen to the Word of God with great respect and attention. I will remember that there is not a sermon in which I may not find something to learn, something to imitate, and something to practise.

PRAYER.—My gracious Lord, grant that I may seek Thee with my whole heart, and know no rest until I have found Thee.

JESUS FEEDS FIVE THOUSAND.

" And taking the five loaves and the two fishes, He looked up to heaven, and blessed them ; and He broke, and distributed to His disciples, to set before the multitude."—St. Luke ix. 16.

INVOCATION.—I beseech Thee, Holy Spirit, help me to understand this solemn scene.

I. The day is on the decline. The eager listeners heed not the lateness of the hour. The slanting rays of the sun are casting a crimson glow over the sea of upturned faces. The little children have fallen asleep in their mother's arms. The compassionate heart of Jesus is moved with pity. He cannot let the people go home fasting, lest they should faint by the way. Turning to the disciples, He says to Philip, "Whence shall we buy bread that these may eat?" Philip, absorbed as usual in pious meditation, replies naïvely, that two hundred pennyworth of bread would not be sufficient for them. Andrew now comes forward, saying that there is a boy present who possesses five loaves and two small fishes, adding, "but what are these amongst so many?" How touching is the familiar intimacy of this little scene, the embarrassment of the disciples, their simple propositions to the Master, and the indulgent kindness of Jesus!

II. And now the Master says, "Make the men sit down." "And they sat down in ranks, by hundreds and fifties." I picture to myself these rows and rows of men, women and children seated upon the grassy sward, the different coloured costumes of the various districts whence they come adding a picturesque beauty to the scene—the disciples waiting beside the Master—and Jesus, His grave, earnest eyes lifted towards heaven with an indescribable expression of gladness in them, blessing the little loaves which He holds in His sacred hands.

III. The disciples approach, and the Master distributes portion after portion, the supply never failing until all had eaten as much as they would. And when they were filled, Jesus said to the disciples, "Gather up the fragments that remain, that nothing be lost." "They gathered up, therefore, and filled twelve baskets with the fragments of the five barley loaves that remained over and above to them that had eaten."

I listen in spirit to the joyful cries of the people, as they praise the miracle. I picture Jesus imposing silence by a gesture and giving His benediction to the multitude. Gradually the vast assemblage melts away and disperses.

I behold in this touching miracle the foreshadowing of the Holy Eucharist. Daily upon the altars of our churches the wonder is repeated. The Sacred Hosts are multiplied. Their supply is divinely inexhaustible. The compassion of Jesus for the souls of men is as ardent as was His pity for the bodily wants of the five thousand. He knows that we should faint by the way in the journey of life, unless He gave us miraculous Food!

RESOLUTION.—The orderly manner in which Jesus commands the multitude to be seated, teaches me the recollected demeanour with which I ought to approach the altar. On great Feasts, when there is much pushing and confusion, I will await my turn patiently and quietly, making way respectfully for those who have already received Holy Communion, and reciting prayers the while in order to prevent my thoughts from being distracted.

PRAYER.—Blessed and praised every moment be the most holy and most divine Sacrament!

JESUS WALKS UPON THE SEA.

"When they had rowed therefore about five and twenty or thirty furlongs, they see Jesus walking upon the sea, and drawing nigh to the ship, and they were afraid."—St. John vi. 19.

INVOCATION.—Oh! my God, I believe in Thee, I hope in Thee, I love Thee!

I. The waters of the usually placid lake are black and angry. Sharp gusts of wind are beating down from the mountains. Thick clouds gather rapidly over the heavens, obscuring the silvery radiance of the moon. A little boat is struggling in the trough of the waters, about mid-way across Gennesareth. The disciples are alone. They are rowing with might and main, but can make little head against the violence of the storm.

Through the darkness they suddenly descry the bright form of a Man walking upon the waters as though they had been dry land. It is the Master; but so terrified are the disciples, and so unhinged by their danger, that they do not recognise the familiar form, and cry out that a phantom is approaching them! Then Jesus speaks: " It is I, be not afraid." Peter, only half reassured, replies, " Lord, if it be Thou, bid me come to Thee upon the waters."

Jesus says "Come." "And Peter, going down out of the boat, walked upon the water to come to Jesus."

But at this moment a violent gust of wind blows, a wave dashes against him. Peter feels himself sinking. He is frightened, and cries out, "Lord, save me." "And immediately Jesus, stretching forth His hand, took hold of him, and said to him, O, thou of little faith, why didst thou doubt?"

II. As the Master takes His place amongst the disciples, the wind goes down. I behold Him standing erect in the boat, which is now gliding softly over the calm surface of the lake. The moon shines out brightly from behind a cloud, and the Apostles fall upon their knees, adoring the Saviour, and exclaiming, "Indeed, Thou art the Son of God!"

Ah! sweetest Lord! how often do those blessed words, "Be not afraid," console and comfort me when my heart is sad and sore! Sorrow comes into my life, or trouble in one shape or another. I am cast down; the pain seems almost more than I can bear. At that moment Thou whisperest in my ear, "Have a good heart; it is I, fear ye not!" It is Jesus Who gives me this suffering, He then will give me also strength to endure it. If death takes from me those whom I love most, and I am left lonely and forlorn upon the tempestuous sea of the unkind world, louder than the dull pain knocking at my heart echo the sweet words, "It is I, be not afraid!"

RESOLUTION.—In moments of danger, in hours of distress, I will take courage from the thought, that be the waves of tribulation rough as they may, Jesus is in their midst, His outstretched hand ready to save me from sinking. In the darkest night of sorrow I will confide in Him, and say "Thy Will be done" with my lips until I can repeat the words from the depths of my heart.

PRAYER.—My Blessed Lord! take me into the shelter of Thine arms, I pray Thee. Grant that I may never leave their holy refuge.

MOUNT TABOR.

"And after six days Jesus taketh with him Peter and James and John, and leadeth them up into a high mountain apart by themselves, and was transfigured before them."— St. Mark ix. 1.

INVOCATION.—I adore Thee, O Jesus, and beseech Thee to enlighten my mind, so that I may know Thee and love Thee.

I. A mountain is before my eyes, rising up in solitary grandeur out of the flowery plain of Esdraelon. Its slopes are covered with the deep green of the myrtle, whilst here and there towers a magnificent oak. From its summit the whole scene of the Saviour's apostolate lies spread out, as it were in a map, at my feet. Nazareth, Cana, Capharnaum, all the cities and villages around the blue lake of Gennesareth. A little farther on is Naim, with Samaria's vast plain stretching away in the distance. Here is Lebanon, with its stately cedars and snowy peaks; there are the dark-reddish mountains of Gergasa; and throughout the fair landscape a silver thread winds in and out, marking the course of the river Jordan. Along one of the shaded paths Jesus is walking with three of His disciples—Peter, James, and John. It is evening. Jesus is retreating to the mountain in order to pray. As He walks along, I fancy I hear Him saying encouraging words to the three, whose hearts are sad, for the Master has been speaking of His approaching death.

II. The Saviour kneels in prayer. The three Apostles have fallen asleep. Suddenly they are awakened by a brilliant light. They open their eyes and behold Jesus, His face shining like the sun, His garments glittering and white as snow, with an expression of majesty upon His countenance which they have never seen before. It is the glory of the Divinity shining through the Sacred Humanity, for the first and last time during His mortal life! On either side of Jesus the astonished disciples behold Moses and Elias, who are " talking " with Him.

My adorable Jesus! I kneel at Thy feet and contemplate Thee with St. John, who, rapt in ecstasy at the sight of his beloved Master in such glory, is gazing upon Thee in silence. The impetuous Peter, scarcely knowing what He says, exclaims: "Master, it is good for us to be here; and let us make three tabernacles, one for Thee, one for Moses, and one for Elias."

Have I never felt as Peter felt? In moments of great fervour, such as at my first Communion, when Jesus came to me for the first time, did I not feel so happy, so strangely different from my usual self, that I almost longed to die, like Blessed Imelda, that I might be for ever thus in His blessed company? But this might not be! Heaven is not to be won so easily. I have work to do. I have self-denial to practise. I have suffering to endure. If Jesus gives me a glimpse of His glory on Tabor, it is to encourage me to seek Him on Calvary. He redeemed me by the Cross, and therefore it is in crosses, and not in sweetnesses, that He will have me love Him.

RESOLUTION.—I resolve, with God's grace, to be equally faithful in His service, whether I find pleasure in my pious exercises or no. On days when my meditation seems dry, my rosary interminable, and my visit to the Blessed Sacrament wearisome—instead of shortening, or omitting anything, I will make it a point of conscience to omit none of these acts of devotion, and will beseech Jesus, out of the treasures of His love, to supply the fervour which is wanting to me.

PRAYER.—I beseech Thee, sweet Lord Jesus, make me faithful in Thy holy service.

MARTHA AND MARY.

"Now it came to pass as they went, that he entered into a certain town; and a certain woman named Martha received Him into her house."—St. Luke x. 38.

INVOCATION.—My Blessed Lord, permit me to remain at Thy feet and listen to Thy holy teaching.

I. I behold Jesus and His disciples approaching the little town of Bethania. It is a peaceful, quiet spot, almost at the gates of Jerusalem, but hidden from view of that city by the luxuriant foliage which encloses it as in a bower. It is especially dear to Jesus, since it is the home of His friends Lazarus, Martha, and Mary Magdalen; and it is here that the Saviour dwells during His visits to Jerusalem, here that He seeks repose beside the tender and devoted hearts of His friends, after His harassing interviews with the Pharisees.

II. I can fancy the delight with which the sisters hail the Master's arrival. Martha, who is head of the house, is all anxiety to do honour to her guests; and after the first words of greeting, hastens away to superintend the preparations for the festive banquet wherewith to welcome Jesus and the Twelve. I picture her to myself hurrying to and fro, giving orders to her servants, and preparing many of the viands with her own deft fingers.

And Mary, where is she? She has forgotten everything but her delight at beholding Jesus! I find her seated at the Master's feet, gazing into His loved face and drinking in every word which falls from His sacred lips.

Martha is vexed that her sister does not come and assist her. After endeavouring, in vain, to attract Mary's attention, she comes up to Jesus and says, "Lord, hast Thou no care that my sister has left me alone to serve? Speak to her, therefore, that she may help me." But Jesus answers, " Martha, Martha, thou art careful and art troubled about many things. But one thing is necessary. Mary has chosen the best part, which shall not be taken away from her."

Jesus does not blame Martha for her active solicitude; He is always grateful for services rendered to Himself; but by His greater praise of Mary, He teaches me the beauty of an interior life. "One thing is necessary," Jesus says. That *one thing* is the salvation of my soul. I cannot spend hours in prayer and meditation. My nature is so frivolous that I can scarcely keep the Presence of God before my mind for five minutes together. And yet I am put into the world, not to please myself, not to amuse myself, not to live for myself, but solely and only to serve, know, and love God; in other words, sanctify my soul. How can I do this? By combining the occupations of the two sisters, by doing every action—no matter whether it be work, play, or prayer, with the intention of pleasing Jesus, and by lifting my heart to Him from time to time with a loving word or thought.

RESOLUTION.—I will venerate the two forms of devotion to our Lord Jesus Christ of which Martha and Mary are the types, in the active and contemplative Orders in whose ranks generations of Saints have adorned the Church.

PRAYER.—Lord Jesus! grant that I may know Thee better, in order to serve Thee more faithfully, and love Thee more ardently.

FEAST OF TABERNACLES.

"Now about the midst of the Feast, Jesus went up into the Temple, and taught."—St. John vii. 14.

INVOCATION.—I adore Thee, most gracious Lord. Enlighten my mind, that I may know Thee and love Thee.

I. The streets of Jerusalem are covered with tents, gracefully fashioned out of the boughs of trees intertwined. In these the vast concourse of pilgrims gathered together for the Feast of Tabernacles are dwelling, in remembrance of the wanderings of the children of Israel through the wilderness. The Name of Jesus is on every lip. His miracles are discussed on all sides. Every Galilean caravan is eagerly scanned on its arrival. The Jews are infuriated against Jesus. Those amongst the people who believe in Him are afraid to express their opinion.

Excitement is at its height when Jesus appears in the Temple. I kneel at the dear Master's feet and listen to His sacred teaching, which becomes more solemn and more full of Divine signification as day follows day. I tremble as I behold the wicked, angry countenances of the Pharisees, whilst they plot with the chief priests how they shall take the life of Jesus.

II. It is the last night of the Feast. I behold the façade of the magnificent Temple brilliantly illuminated; two gigantic candelabra light up the whole town with the splendour of their rays. Jesus takes the opportunity of teaching the people by this familiar symbol that He is the Light of the World. The fury of the Pharisees knows no bounds, and they send soldiers to seize the Master, that they may put Him to death.

What a scene is before my eyes! The meek Saviour, calm and unmoved in the midst of His enemies, His sweet grave voice rising steadily above the angry tones of the Jews. The pilgrims whom He is teaching listen reverently to His holy words, but look round furtively from time to time, as the tumult amongst the Jews increases. And now I behold a band of soldiers making their way stealthily behind the crowd. They pause and listen for a moment. The majesty and sweetness of the Saviour disarm these men. "Never did man speak like this Man," they say! The plan of arrest has failed. But the life of Jesus is in hourly danger, and, as His hour has not yet come, He leaves Jerusalem and takes refuge in a quiet sequestered district on the banks of the Jordan.

My beloved Lord, I follow Thee as Thou escapest from Thine enemies. I kneel at Thy feet in the solitude wherein Thou dost take shelter, and beseech Thee to teach me by Thy Divine example to bear persecution and unkindness meekly and patiently, when they fall to my lot.

I suffer for my faith perhaps; or else I am simply trying to lead a better life, to break with old habits and give up bad companionship. On this account I have to endure a storm of petty persecution. How do I behave on such occasions? Do I persevere steadily in well-doing? or do I angrily retaliate upon my tormentors, returning hard word for hard word, sneer for sneer?

RESOLUTION.—Whenever my heart is full of anger at the injustice under which I am smarting, I. will think of my God, forced to hide from His enemies, and beseech Him, by His Divine sweetness, to remove all bitterness from my heart.

PRAYER.—I pray Thee, adorable Jesus, have pity on all my enemies, and do good to those who have done evil to me.

TWO BLIND MEN.

"And behold two blind men sitting by the wayside, heard that Jesus passed by, and they cried out, saying: O Lord, Thou Son of David, have mercy on us."— St. Matt. xx. 30.

INVOCATION.—O Jesus, by the compassion of Thy Divine Heart, have pity on me, I beseech Thee.

I. I contemplate my dear Saviour in His peaceful retreat amongst the simple-minded inhabitants of Perea. I watch His steps, as He walks from village to village, comforting the sorrowful, healing the sick, teaching the ignorant, and blessing the little children who, as usual, flock in His path.

One day Jesus leaves His seclusion to visit Jericho. As He leaves the town, a multitude of people follow Him. On the outskirts I perceive two blind men, beggars in all probability, sitting by the roadside. They hear the steps of the crowd and the hum of many voices. The name of *Jesus* falls on their ear. It is Jesus, then, Who is passing by! Immediately the two poor men begin to cry out loudly, "O Lord, Thou Son of David, have mercy on us!" The people rebuke them. "The Master has passed," I fancy I hear them say; "is it likely He will turn back for such as you?" etc., etc.

But the poor afflicted creatures are not to be silenced, and they cry out the louder, "O Lord, Thou Son of David, have mercy on us!"

II. Jesus hears the cries and the uncharitable remarks of the people. A look of pity comes over His sweet, grave face. He stops, and calls the two blind men to Him. I can fancy the eagerness with which they obey the call, guiding themselves by their hands through the crowd to the Saviour. "What will ye that I do to you?" Jesus asks them. "They say to Him, Lord, that our eyes be opened. And Jesus, having compassion on them, touched their eyes, and immediately they saw, and followed Him."

How wonderful, how beautiful is the compassion of Jesus! An unkind word, two poor sightless beggars rudely bidden be silent, and a miracle of tenderness is performed! He has enemies on all sides. His miracles are called in question. His doctrine is contradicted. He is even proclaimed as an impostor. The very crowds which are following Him will soon take part against Him; and yet His pity, His love, His compassion never vary! As the sun shines upon the evil and the good alike, so does Jesus shower blessings upon the grateful and the ungrateful; He makes no distinctions.

What a lesson is here for me! When my motives are misjudged, when those to whom I have shown affection treat me with ingratitude or disdain, how do I behave? Do I accept their unkindness patiently and meekly, seeking how to render them service in return, with as much zeal as though they had been amiable towards me?

Does the sight of misery or suffering always call forth my sympathy and compassion?

RESOLUTION.—In rendering kindnesses or services, I will not look for gratitude or a return for my affection. I will seek out those who are the least amiable and prepossessing of my fellow-creatures, and who in consequence have few friends, and endeavour by my charity and amiability to work the miracle of softening their harsh, repellent natures, for the love of Jesus.

PRAYER.—Most merciful Jesus, I pray Thee, help me by Thy grace to keep these my resolutions.

DEATH OF LAZARUS.

"His sisters therefore sent to Him, saying: Lord, behold, he whom Thou lovest is sick."—St. John xi. 3.

INVOCATION.—I beseech Thee, sweetest Lord, increase my faith and strengthen my hope in Thee.

I. I behold a messenger advancing towards Jesus in hot haste. He is sent by Martha and Mary with the few but expressive words, "He whom Thou lovest is sick."

The disciples are dismayed when they find that the Master is preparing to go to Bethania. They seek to dissuade Him from His project, urging that but lately the Jews sought to stone Him, and that He is incurring peril of death if He ventures into Judea again. But Jesus loves Martha and Mary and Lazarus. He is their friend, and He will not remain absent from them in their anxiety and affliction.

What a lesson is contained for me in this devotion of Jesus to His friends! I have need to remember that to visit those who are in affliction is Christ-like; for alas, when my friends are ill or suffering, it costs me a struggle to sacrifice my own pleasure and to remain by their bedside, helping to cheer the long, tedious hours of sickness!

II. The Saviour approaches Bethania. Far away in the distance Martha has seen His familiar form. She rushes to meet Him with the sorrowful reproach on her lips, "Lord, if Thou hadst been here, my brother had not died." For Lazarus is dead! The sisters had hoped to the last that Jesus would come in time to save His friend. They had full confidence in His tenderness. But four days elapsed and Jesus came not—Lazarus is not only dead, but buried!

As I watch the Saviour, His sweet face testifying the sorrow He feels at Martha's sad tidings, I fancy that His eyes seek some one. Martha notices the look, hastens back to the house which she had left in her eagerness to meet the Master, and goes in search of Mary, telling her that "the Master is come and calleth for thee." Mary rises at once, followed by a crowd of mourners who are with her in the house, and throwing herself at the feet of Jesus, weeps bitterly. At the sight of Magdalen's grief, oh, miracle of tenderness! Jesus weeps also. He asks where have they laid Lazarus? "They say to Him, Lord, come and see."

III. I follow the Master and the two sorrowing sisters as, with the crowd of mourners, they thread the terraces and alleys of their beautiful garden to the sepulchre where the dead brother has been laid.

Ah, my sweet Lord, where shall I find a friend on earth like Thee! Thou sympathizest, lovest, reprovest, consolest, and dost not hesitate to impose a cross upon those Whom Thou lovest best. Is not this friendship a type of the guide of my soul, the holy friend to whom I may pour out all my miseries, all my weaknesses, all my trials and sorrows, sure of sympathy, counsel, and help?

RESOLUTION.—I will say a prayer daily for my confessor, beseeching God to help him in his arduous work of sanctifying my soul, and to make me obedient and docile to his holy direction.

PRAYER.—O Jesus, thou Friend of friends! fill my heart with Thy love, I entreat Thee.

RESURRECTION OF LAZARUS.

"When He had said these things, he cried with a loud voice: Lazarus, come forth."—St. John xi. 43.

INVOCATION.—My Divine Lord, grant that I may never be deaf to Thy voice, I beseech Thee.

I. Jesus is standing before the cave which contains the body of Lazarus. A large stone has been placed at the entrance, as a door. Jesus orders that the stone be removed. At this Martha rushes forward. She wishes to spare Jesus a painful sight. Lazarus has been dead for four days, "by this time he stinketh," she says. But Jesus gently insists. The stone is rolled away.

As I gaze into the gloomy tomb, the thought of my own death comes to my mind. I know not how long I have yet to live. Death comes at all ages. A spark of fire, a stone, a fall, a thousand things, trifling in themselves, may put an end to my existence at any moment. Do I ever think of this? If I did, how holy would be my life! It would not need to be outwardly different. All God requires of me is to commit no sin wilfully, to obey Him, to love Him with all my might, and to go to my every action with the intention of pleasing Him. Perfection does not consist in great deeds, but in great faithfulness in doing all things well, for the love of God!

II. Jesus cried with a loud voice, "Lazarus, come forth!" I picture the scene to myself. The Master standing erect, His beautiful countenance suddenly glowing with a Divine radiance. The weeping sisters, on hearing those wonderful words, start and look eagerly towards the sepulchre. The disciples and the by-standers press forward. Expectation is written on every face.

III. "And presently, he that had been dead came forth, bound feet and hands with winding-bands, and his face was bound about with a napkin." Jesus said to them, "Loose him, and let him go."

Joyfully, indeed, do Martha and Mary obey this order, their fingers trembling with the intensity of their emotion as they undo the tight wrappings in which their brother had been shrouded. And now, as Lazarus, having recovered the freedom of his limbs, throws himself at the feet of Jesus, the crowd of mourners bursts forth into a cry of admiration and rapture at the miracle.

What is the lesson I carry home from this marvellous scene? Surely the resurrection of the friend of Jesus is a type of my soul when restored to new life by grace. I commit a venial fault. The beauty of my soul is tarnished. An act of contrition would wipe away the stain. But alas! I do not heed the voice of conscience. Fault follows fault until the shining purity is all dimmed and marred. But Jesus has mercy on me! His loving voice whispers in my ear. He bids me "Come forth" from my indifference, from my hard impenitence.

RESOLUTION.—Jesus shall not call me in vain. I will kneel at His feet in the tribunal of Penance and ask Him to give absolution to my soul, and accept me as His repentant, humble child.

PRAYER.—Most Gracious Lord, I offer Thee every hour of my future life. Grant that I may never offend Thee wilfully again, I implore Thee.

JESUS RIDES INTO JERUSALEM UPON A COLT.

"And when they were drawing near to Jerusalem and to Bethania at the mount of olives, He sendeth two of His disciples, and saith to them : Go into the village that is over against you, and immediately at your coming in thither, you shall find a colt tied, upon which no man yet hath sat : loose him, and bring him. . . . And they brought the colt to Jesus ; and they laid their garments on him, and He sat upon him."—St. Mark xi. 1, 2, 7.

INVOCATION.—My God, grant me a teachable heart, I pray Thee, and the grace of recollection.

I. In the early morning, Jesus leaves the house of Lazarus, and, accompanied by His disciples, directs His steps towards Jerusalem. His Mother trembles at the thought of His entering that city filled with enemies. Lazarus, Martha and Mary gaze wistfully after Him as His beloved form disappears from their sight, their hearts heavy with sad forebodings.

Not death, however, but a peaceful triumph awaits the Saviour this day.

II. On reaching the village of Bethphage, Jesus sends two of His disciples to fetch the colt on which He desires to make His entry into the great city. Happy colt, to be the bearer of such a burthen ! I watch the disciples as they loose the halter which fastens the gentle beast to a gateway, and throwing their cloaks across his back, lead him to the Master. He is unbroken; he has never carried anyone; but now, as he meekly bears the Saviour upon his back, I fancy that he knows his Creator, and is proud of the honour conferred on him—the humblest of all domestic animals.

There is a hidden lesson for me in this lowly choice of Jesus. It tells me that when I have some little triumph in prospect—an examination, perhaps, or some such opportunity of receiving commendation and applause, I must make a provision of modesty beforehand, in order not to wound the feelings of others. I must make those who are less gifted, or less successful than myself, *forgive my superiority.* Do I do this? Does not my face, on the contrary, by its proud, exultant expression, betray my self-consciousness?

Our Blessed Lord loves the meek and humble of heart. He tells me so by every action of His life, and especially by choosing the meekest and most abject of all beasts of burden on which to make His triumphal entry into Jerusalem. How, then, can He love me, when I am so proud, so filled with self-esteem, so wanting in modesty and in charity towards my neighbour!

RESOLUTION.—I will observe myself closely for the future, and whenever I find that I am in danger of displaying my superiority, I will think of Jesus riding on a colt, the foal of an ass. I will convert my superiority into a means of practising the virtue of charity, by placing my talents at the service of those who are less intelligent than myself, helping them in their difficulties, and taking more pride in their success than in my own.

PRAYER.—Oh, Jesus! meek and humble of heart. Teach me my own nothingness, I pray Thee. Make my heart like Thine!

HOSANNA!

"And a very great multitude spread their garments in the way, and others cut boughs from the trees and strewed them in the way. And the multitudes that went before, and that followed, cried, saying: Hosanna to the son of David: blessed is He that cometh in the name of the Lord! Hosanna in the highest!"—St. Matt. xxi. 8, 9.

INVOCATION.—Blessed Lord, I unite my heart to the praises of the multitude. Teach me to do Thy will in preference to my own.

I. As Jesus draws near to the city, a rumour of his approach spreads amongst the multitude of people who have come to Jerusalem to celebrate the Pasch. Amongst these are many who have followed the Saviour in His apostolic journeys, have listened to His teachings, and have witnessed His miracles.

Hearing that the Great Prophet is at the city-gate, men, women, and children flock to meet Him, carrying palm-branches and olive-boughs in their hands.* The air rings with their acclamations. They accompany Him in a joyous triumphant procession, bestrewing the ground with their garments and green branches. "Hosanna! Hosanna!" they cry. "Hosanna in the highest!"

* The carrying of green boughs was a customary expression of great joy on the part of the Jewish people.

II. The sacred countenance of Jesus, meanwhile, is grave with a pathetic sweetness. I can almost fancy I see tears in His loving eyes. He is ready to weep over these multitudes who are now praising Him as their King, and who, a few days hence, will lead Him to a shameful death. His heart is sad as He passes through the streets which will so soon be watered with His blood. His Passion is before Him, but He stays not. He does not turn aside. With all the docility of a meek lamb, of which He is the Divine figure, He goes on to His doom without a thought of resistance. His obedience is perfect.

What a lesson—what an example to me is this obedience of Jesus! Jesus has obeyed all His life. As He obeyed Mary and Joseph, when a child, so now He obeys His heavenly Father. And for whose sake does He thus obey? For mine! I must obey even as Jesus obeyed, for I am His child and must resemble Him, else He will not own me. It is not enough to execute the wishes of my parents, or of those who hold their place, slowly, grudgingly, regretfully. I must obey promptly, generously, as Jesus obeyed.

RESOLUTION.—When it costs me a struggle to put aside my own wishes, or my own judgment (as, alas! it so frequently does), when my heart is rebellious, and I feel irritated and angered with those who enforce my submission, I will think of the meek, gentle Saviour going so obediently to death for my sake, and then surely I shall find it less hard to obey; surely my heart will be stirred to some little act of generosity for the sake of Him who is about to shed all His blood for me!

PRAYER.—My Blessed Lord! I give Thee my heart. Make it docile and obedient, I beseech Thee. Grant that it may become an image of Thy Heart. Mother Mary! by the obedience of thy Son, help me to be obedient, I beseech thee.

THE CENACLE.

"And He sent Peter and John, saying: Go and prepare for us the Pasch, that we may eat. . . . And when the hour was come, He sat down and the twelve Apostles with Him."—St. Luke xxii. 8, 14.

INVOCATION.—My Blessed Saviour, accept my love, I entreat Thee. Grant that I may follow closely in Thy steps.

I. The hour draws near when Jesus is about to be delivered up into the hands of His enemies. According to Jewish custom, all families meet together at a certain date every year at Jerusalem to celebrate the Pasch. Jesus, therefore, sends two of His disciples into the city to prepare for the Feast, and directs them to the house of a wealthy Jew, supposed to have been Nicodemus. The two disciples chosen are Peter, the type of faith; and John, the type of love.

II. It is night. The Apostles have done as Jesus commanded. The guest-room is a long upper chamber, hung with silken draperies, on which emblems of the Paschal ceremonies are embroidered. Curiously wrought lamps are suspended from the roof, and precious perfumes are burning in enormous censers at the four corners. A long table, covered with a fine linen cloth, occupies the centre, upon which the Apostles have laid their modest provisions for the Feast—the Paschal lamb, some loaves of unleavened bread, and several bowls filled with a bitter kind of lettuce.

III. I will join the little band of holy women whom tradition tells me are in an adjoining chamber, and contemplate the actions of my Saviour.

I behold the meek, majestic figure of Jesus seated at the table, surrounded by His Apostles.

Judas is there. The secret of his treachery is known to none but his Master, Whose eyes rest sorrowfully upon him from time to time. As if it were to give him a chance of repentance, Jesus says sadly: "One of you is about to betray Me." At these words the Apostles look from one to the other, consternation depicted on their countenances. What! they who love Jesus so ardently! Can it be possible they shall betray Him? Each eagerly asks, "Is it I, Lord?" And Judas, whose malice is not disarmed by the tender look of his Master, joins with the others in asking, "Is it I, Lord?" Jesus answers him in a low voice, so as to spare him the shame of being recognised as the traitor by the other disciples, "Thou hast said it." How compassionate is Jesus! How considerate towards the faithless disciple whose falseness must have pierced him to the heart!

This conduct of my Saviour teaches me how I ought to behave towards unfaithful friends, and towards those who are unkind or ungrateful to me. Too often, when I meet with coldness where I expected affection, or neglect and perhaps even treachery from those whom I considered my friends, I complain bitterly of their injustice. My heart grows hard towards them, and I pass them by with a haughty look, or mutter a vindictive remark loud enough for them to hear.

RESOLUTION.—Whenever this happens, I will remember the treason of Judas, and confess myself unworthy to be treated otherwise than was my Lord. I will try to overcome evil with good. I will be amiable and forgiving towards those who are unkind to me, and will try to win their hearts by my sweetness. Why, indeed, should I be surprised when I find myself disliked? Am I so amiable, so perfect, that everyone should be forced to love me?

PRAYER.—My kind Saviour! Thou wilt ever be my faithful Friend. Grant that I may always love Thee, never do anything to offend Thee, and for Thy sake forgive all injuries.

JESUS WASHES THE DISCIPLES' FEET.

"He riseth from supper, and layeth aside His garments, and having taken a towel, girded Himself."
—St. John xiii. 4.

INVOCATION.—I beseech Thee, my beloved Lord, enlighten my mind that I may understand and follow Thy Divine teachings.

I. The Jewish ceremony of the Pasch is over. And now Jesus, having fulfilled the old law, is about to institute a new Sacrifice—the Sacrifice of His love—and give His disciples a still greater proof of His tenderness than any they have hitherto received. The hearts of the Twelve are heavy, for the Master has spoken to them frequently of late of His death, and, from His words during the Paschal Supper, they feel that it is near. I can see the gentle, loving St. John clinging closer and closer to the Master, as though he dreaded a sudden separation, and St. Peter and the others anxiously studying the beloved Face which has hitherto been the key to all their confidence, all their strength.

II. Now the Saviour rises from the table, and laying aside the long woollen robe or cloak which He wore in common with all Jews, He pours some water into a basin, and, girding a towel round His waist, meekly kneels down upon the floor before each disciple, and proceeds to wash the feet of all. According to Eastern custom the Apostles are half-sitting, half-reclining upon couches round the supper-table. Oh, my Jesus, what a spectacle do I behold ! The Lord of heaven and earth bends down before His creatures ! With a tenderness infinitely touching to behold, the God of all purity bathes the dusty, travel-stained feet of twelve poor men with His own sacred Hands !

Oh, my Jesus, when I contemplate Thee, so adorably humble, how can I refuse to lay all my own miserable pride and fastidiousness at Thy feet ? Grant me, I beseech Thee, true humility. Grant that I may rejoice whenever I have an opportunity of proving my love to Thee, and of imitating Thee by rendering services to my neighbour which are repugnant to my natural feelings.

III. The Apostles are astonished and puzzled beyond measure at this action on the part of the Master. Why, their countenances ask, should Jesus act thus towards them, His lowly followers ? St. Peter eagerly protests against such a humiliation on the part of his beloved Lord. Drawing his feet quickly under his robe, "Thou shalt never wash my feet !" he exclaims. Jesus gently constrains him with the words, "If I wash thee not, thou shalt have no part with Me."

This teaching of the Saviour to St. Peter points out to me the lesson I must draw from the scene I have just witnessed. It shows me the purity with which I must approach Holy Communion, rendering my heart spotless before I dare to present myself at the Holy Table. It is not enough that my conscience be free from the filth of great sins: it must be cleansed also from the dust of those little every-day faults and imperfections which I am too apt to overlook or to consider too small and insignificant to trouble myself about. I say, in my indolence, sometimes, "I shall never be a saint. Enough for me if I avoid great sins. I cannot pretend to perfection." And yet, if I truly love Jesus, how shall I bear to receive Him into a heart sullied with even the semblance of a stain?

RESOLUTION.—I will examine my conscience more carefully than I have hitherto done when preparing for Confession. I will pray fervently that God will help me to know my faults; and I will endeavour to conquer my natural indolence, and to acquire the virtues in which I am now so sadly wanting.

PRAYER.—Blessed Lord! Help me to excite in my heart a more sincere and earnest sorrow for my offences against Thee.

THE LAST SUPPER.

"And whilst they were at supper, Jesus took bread, and blessed, and broke: and gave to His disciples, and said: Take ye, and eat: This is My body. And taking the chalice He gave thanks: and gave to them, saying: Drink ye all of this. For this is My blood of the new testament which shall be shed for many unto remission of sins."—St. Matt. xxvi. 26—28.

INVOCATION.—Oh, my beloved Jesus! Open my eyes, I beseech Thee, that I may understand the tenderness of Thy love. Purify my heart, I pray Thee, that it may be worthy of being Thy dwelling.

I. Silence reigns over the city. The noise and bustle of the Jewish Feast is at an end, and the inhabitants have dispersed to their homes. The surrounding stillness makes the night appear doubly solemn to the little band assembled in the Cenacle.

After washing His disciples' feet, Jesus once more seats Himself at the table in their midst. The Twelve little dream of the new and touching feast which is in store for them. They are strangely moved by the unwonted tenderness of the Master. There is a look upon His grave, beautiful countenance which they do not understand, and which saddens them, they know not why. His words are so loving, their hearts melt as they hear Him speak.

II. The Saviour now takes a piece of unleavened bread in His hands. He raises His eyes to heaven, as if thanking His Eternal Father in the name of all mankind for the precious gift He is about to bestow; then, gazing at the morsel of bread which is to be the object of such a miracle, He blesses it with that right hand which sustains the world. "Take ye, and eat," Jesus says, with an indefinable expression of love and joy in His voice; "this is My Body. And taking the chalice, He gave thanks, and gave to them, saying, Drink ye all of this, for this is My Blood."

I can fancy I behold the Angels prostrating themselves in adoration at this moment, whilst Jesus—with a majesty, with a reverence, with a deep recollectedness impossible to describe —goes from one dear disciple to another, communicating them all with His own hand, feeding them with that heavenly Food, showing them indeed that He "loved them unto the end."

Oh, my beloved Lord! Upon my knees, in humblest worship, I thank Thee for this Thy love. What return can I make for a love so great? "My child," I hear Thee say, "give Me thy heart." Jesus asks me to come to Him, to come to His Altar, where daily He gives Himself as Food for our souls. He condescends to *ask*—He, Jesus, the Son of the living God! O Jesus, grant that I may never disappoint Thee, never refuse Thee admittance into my heart! Grant that my greatest happiness on earth may be this blessed union with Thee!

RESOLUTION.—In order to prepare my heart for the coming of Jesus, I will imitate St. Catharine of Siena, and build a little cell therein, where I may retire frequently and converse with Jesus. I will make Him an altar there, on which I will offer up my own will, my faults, and especially my besetting sin. It shall have the virtue of purity for its white cloth. I will decorate it with flowers whose fragrance Jesus loves—the virtues of modesty, humility, patience, and devotion; whilst the lamp which hangs before it shall be lit with love of Jesus in the Blessed Sacrament, and fed with the oil of charity towards my neighbour.

PRAYER.—Holy St. Catharine, out of the riches of your great love, help me, I pray you, to receive Jesus reverently and devoutly in Holy Communion, and teach me to serve Him better, day by day.

THE AGONY IN THE GARDEN.

" And going out, He went according to His custom to the mount of olives. And His disciples also followed Him."—St. Luke xxii. 39.

INVOCATION.—My afflicted Lord, grant me, I pray Thee, true sorrow for my sins, which caused Thee such grief.

I. After the institution of the Holy Eucharist, Jesus rises from table and leads His disciples towards the Mount of Olives. The night is still. The moon is shining brightly, and by its light the Apostles perceive that the Master's face is sorrowful beyond words.

Their hearts are heavy and uneasy with an indefinable presentiment of coming separation, as they follow their Lord through the Valley of Josaphat, across the torrent of Cedron, to the olive-covered mountain they know so well. Part of the mount is enclosed within walls, and is called the Garden of Gethsemani. It is thickly planted with trees and shrubs, and contains several caverns and secluded nooks, suitable for quiet solitary prayer.

II. At the entrance to the enclosure, Jesus takes Peter, James, and John with Him, and leaves the other disciples outside the low wall which separates the Garden from the rest of the mountain. Bidding these three keep watch, I behold my Saviour enter one of the caves. Kneeling down, He begins to pray. And what a prayer! It is the Agony of Jesus! The Agony of God made man. A great fear of His death, with all the horrors of His Passion, afflicts His soul. His heart is wrung with anguish as He beholds the sins and ingratitude of mankind unrolled before Him in, as it were, a long, terrible succession of pictures. A deep sadness oppresses Him as He sees how little love He will receive for the ocean of charity which He is pouring out upon the world.

Nature at last gives way under such an intensity of suffering, and Jesus falls upon His face before His Father, incensed against Him on account of our sins, with which He has clothed Himself! Never on earth was there such sadness. Beads of blood stand upon His sacred brow; a sweat of blood bursts from His veins until His very garments are saturated, as the large drops roll down His face, suffuse His limbs, and stain the white dust upon which He is lying prostrate!

Oh, my God! my Jesus! make me feel compassion for Thy anguish! Permit me to kneel down by Thy side, and adore Thee in this solitary cavern. Thou art alone; Thy disciples are asleep. I see Thee rise, and Thy tender Heart is pained by this neglect of theirs. They are tired and exhausted with the weight of their sorrowful forebodings; but Thou tenderly reproachest them: "Could you not watch with Me one hour?" Thou sayest. Sweet Lord, I cannot console Thee in Thy loneliness, but I will creep to Thy feet and offer Thee all my love, poor as it is, and all the sorrows and afflictions which shall befall me in my future life. Look not at the smallness of the gift, I pray Thee; but give me more love to offer Thee in Thy desolation.

RESOLUTION.—When I am inclined to hurry over my prayers, or to shorten the time allotted to my meditation, I will turn my thoughts to Gethsemani, and take home the lesson of perseverance in prayer of which my Saviour gave me such a touching example when, "being in an agony, He prayed the longer."

PRAYER.—By the merit of Thy sufferings in the Garden, I beseech Thee, dear Lord, grant me the grace to love prayer.

JESUS IS TAKEN PRISONER.

"And he that betrayed Him had given them a sign, saying: Whomsoever I shall kiss, that is He."—St. Mark xiv. 44.

INVOCATION.—Touch my heart, I beseech Thee, oh Lord, and fill it with sorrow and contrition.

I. Whilst Jesus is still upon His knees in the Garden, the stillness of the night is disturbed by the tramping of armed men and the clanking of steel. Torches gleam through the gnarled and twisted branches of the olive-trees, and throw a red, fitful light upon the silvery lining of their leaves.

It is Judas the traitor, followed by the troop of soldiers which the high priests have given him for the execution of his perfidious design. He advances towards his kind Master, and with a kiss delivers Him up to death! Jesus does not seek to escape from His enemies. His meek eyes look reproachfully upon Judas as He murmurs, "Friend, whereto art thou come?"

II. The insolent soldiery now rush upon the Saviour. Like a pack of ravenous wolves they seize Him, and bind Him with cords. And the innocent Lamb of God opens not His mouth, but meekly gives Himself up to their violence, suffering their brutality with the same Divine patience as He had suffered the infamous lips of Judas to touch His cheek—He Who, by one word, might crush them into dust!

And the eleven disciples, where are they? Alas! terrified, almost distraught with fear, they fled from their Master at the first sign of danger, and shrinking into the shadow of the mountain, they hid themselves in its caves and thickets. Jesus is alone, in the power of his bloodthirsty, relentless foes!

III. Oh, my Lord! permit me to follow Thee as Thou art roughly dragged down those steep mountain-paths! I shudder at the cruel way in which they pull Thee along, without pause or mercy, through the torrent, even unto Jerusalem. Thy garments are torn and disordered by the brambles, Thy knees are bruised by Thy falls, Thy feet wounded and bleeding from the sharp stones over which they drag Thee so hurriedly! I kiss those sacred hands so tightly and cruelly pinioned behind Thy back! I worship Thy sacred head, uncovered, and bowed down by the exhaustion of so violent a march!

Thou, who art innocent, art bound; and I, who am guilty, am free! And what use do I make of my freedom? My hands, are they constantly employed in Thy service? my steps, are they directed to the fulfilment of my duties? my heart, is it placed where Thou wouldst have it placed?

I think myself free when no one thwarts me, when I follow the gratification of my own desires. Restraint vexes me; rules and regulations fret and annoy me; the wise advice of superiors irritates me. I do not see that, were it not for these irksome restraints which I foolishly imagine fetter my liberty, I should soon fall into a slavery a thousand-fold worse than the gentle submission demanded of me. I should become a slave to myself and to my own evil passions, which would lead me into every kind of danger, temptation, and difficulty, perhaps even into mortal sin.

RESOLUTION.—Whenever I feel disposed to murmur and rebel against authority, against rule, against the spirit of order, I will remember that woful night on the Mount of Olives. When temptation presses me sorely, when pride revolts, and submission seems almost beyond my strength, I will beg Jesus to encircle my heart with those cords which pinioned His precious hands, and to hold my rebellious passions and unruly tongue captive, until the danger is past and my soul once more at peace.

PRAYER.—Bind me so closely to Thee, I beseech Thee, sweet Lord, that I may never be able to leave Thy side. May I rather die than lose Thy grace, my God and my all!

HUMILIATIONS OF JESUS.

" And the chief priests and the whole council sought false-witness against Jesus, that they might put Him to death. . . . Then did they spit in His face, and buffet Him, and others struck his face with the palms of their hands, saying : Prophesy unto us, O Christ ; who is he that struck Thee?"—St. Matt. xxvi. 59, 67, 68.

"Who, when He was reviled, did not revile : when He suffered, He threatened not : but delivered Himself to Him that judged Him unjustly."—1 Peter ii. 23.

INVOCATION.—My God, I beseech Thee, give me grace to meditate upon the humiliations of my Saviour.

I. The suffering Jesus is now inhumanly dragged through the streets of Jerusalem from one tribunal to another. He is taken before Annas, Caiaphas, Herod, and Pilate. I follow Him. His steps are feeble; His strength is well-nigh spent with the brutal treatment He has already received; His hands are bound; a cord is about His neck, and He is led as a criminal from one judge to another. Not a friend is near Him; not a kind look is bent upon His meek, sorrowful countenance. He is alone, defenceless, in the midst of a fierce, angry crowd. Oh, my Jesus! how grievous must this solitude have been to Thy loving heart! I, at least, will bear Thee company, and compassionate Thee in Thy abandonment. I mix with the throng and follow Jesus into the council chambers of Caiaphas, where He is accused of many abominable crimes. Loud and vehement are the tones of the false witnesses, but the innocent Saviour answers not a word.

II. A terrible scene ensues. Jesus is given over into the hands of a troop of vile soldiery and domestics. The Holy of Holies becomes the sport of a cruel, relentless crowd, who, under the cloak of religious zeal, cover Him with indignities, and heap humiliations upon His head, striking Him, buffeting Him, and spitting upon His sacred face. The countenance of Jesus is so venerable, so modest and beautiful, in spite of its disfigurement, that it troubles His tormentors, and they tie a bandage over His face, lest the majesty of His eyes should strike remorse into their hearts. Insult now follows insult, blow succeeds blow, and Jesus is still silent. A sigh every now and again escapes His lips; but not a protest, not a threat, not a murmur. Like an innocent lamb He bears all, suffers all, without so much as a plaint, offering His tortures to the Eternal Father for the pardon of my sins.

Oh, my beloved Saviour! How adorable art Thou in Thy abasement! Permit me to kneel at Thy feet and learn the lessons of meekness and humility which Thou dost so sweetly and so touchingly teach me.

Thou submittest to be made the sport of a vile mob, and I am so proud, so haughty, that I cannot brook a word of good-natured raillery, much less contempt! Thou art falsely accused, and Thou keepest silence; whereas I, at the slightest rebuke, or disparaging remark on my conduct, burst forth into a torrent of self-justification!

RESOLUTION.—From this day forth I resolve to bear all injuries and false accusations patiently and humbly, and by God's grace to stifle every feeling of resentment towards the person at whose hands I have to endure them. I will not seek to justify myself at the expense of another, when accused of a fault which I have not committed, but will bear the accusation as penance for the many faults which I have committed, and of which I have never been accused. I resolve also to do any kindness in my power to those who have injured me, and to pray for them.

PRAYER.—My beloved Jesus! By the merits of Thy humiliations, I beseech Thee make me humble, and teach me to love those who despise and misjudge me, for Thy sake.

DENIAL OF PETER.

"And the Lord, turning, looked on Peter."—St. Luke xxii. 61.

INVOCATION.—My Blessed Jesus; I desire to seek Thee, to follow Thee, and to love Thee with my whole heart.

I. A number of servants are gathered together round a fire in the vestibule of the high priest's house. They are talking and laughing over the trial of Jesus. Timidly and almost furtively, a stranger joins the group, as though to warm his hands. His face is sad, and bears traces of tears. The suspicions of the noisy group are aroused, and looking attentively at Peter, for it is he, they recognise him by his dress as one of the disciples of Jesus. "This man also was with Him," they say. Peter, alarmed, denies any knowledge of his Lord!

Oh, Peter, Peter! Is this the end of thy fervent protestations of love, when thou didst declare thyself ready to go to prison and to death with Jesus? Alas! the self-confident disciple had slept in the Garden of Gethsemani, when he should have watched and prayed with his Master. He had been a coward, and had fled! He had followed

Jesus at a distance, instead of keeping close to his Lord, so as to be strengthened by His grace.

What a lesson is here for me! If Peter, the Prince of the Apostles, is capable of denying his Master in a moment of fear, of what cowardice am not I capable? I make great promises to my Lord, when I am kneeling at His feet before the Blessed Sacrament. I think that I am strong, and proof against all fears. And then, hardly perhaps have I left His Sacred Presence, when a word of ridicule is sufficient to put all my valour to flight! I live in a Protestant country. My friends and relations are, many of them, Protestants—inclined to sneer at the practices of our holy religion. When they do this, am I true to my standard? am I faithful to Jesus? Or do I weakly strive to hide any open manifestation of my faith—in other words, deny Jesus? Do my cheeks tingle when I am laughed at for doing my duty as a Catholic, and do I indignantly disclaim the epithet of "pious," which ought to be my glory? Am I ashamed of making the sign of the Cross when curious eyes are upon me? Of abstaining from meat when my conduct will expose me to unpleasant remarks? If I do this, I am ashamed of Jesus Christ. I am denying Him with St. Peter!

III. Three times the Apostle repeats his denial. And now, with an appearance of boldness, he glances through the open door. Jesus turns His head. He speaks not, but His eyes, filled with a sorrowful compassion, rest upon Peter. In a moment that merciful look melts the disciple's heart. He remembers the prophecy which Jesus had made of his weakness, and bursting into tears, he rushes from the court in an agony of grief and remorse.

Oh, Jesus! when I forget Thee, when I am tempted to deny Thee, of Thy mercy turn Thine eyes upon me! Make me humble, make me diffident of myself, so that my sorrow and contrition may be the foundation of a faith as firm as that for which St. Peter laid down his life!

RESOLUTION.—I will examine myself carefully upon the occasions in which I am likely to deny my Lord and my holy Faith. Instead of trusting in my own strength and courage, I will begin the day by acknowledging my weakness, and by asking Jesus for the strength of His grace.

PRAYER.—Oh, Jesus! have pity on my frailty, and when I am in danger of forgetting Thee, turn upon me the eyes of Thy love.

SCOURGING OF JESUS.

"Then, therefore, Pilate took Jesus and scourged Him."—St. John xix. 1.

INVOCATION.—I beseech Thee, my beloved Lord, grant that my heart may be filled with love and compunction, in contemplating Thy sufferings.

I. It is morning, and the Prætorium is thronged with Jews, clamouring for the death of Jesus, who is again brought before Pilate. That inhuman judge knows that He is innocent, but thinks to appease the fury of the people by ordering their Victim to be scourged.

Jesus is led forth into an outer court, in the centre of which there is a pillar. He is left to the mercy of the Roman soldiers and hirelings. I behold my loving Lord, at the command of these men, obediently divesting himself of His garments, and clasping the pillar with both hands. The executioners bind those sacred hands, and then begins the cruel torture. I kneel in a corner of the court. The sight is almost more than I can bear. Angels must weep for compassion as Jesus stands, with head bent down, eyes meekly cast upon the ground, awaiting the strokes which are to tear His innocent flesh.

II. The executioners are men of stalwart frame and ferocious countenance. I see them approach my Lord armed with scourges. Heavy strokes fall on His back, His shoulders, His legs—even His sacred Face is not spared! The scourges are full of blood. The column is wet with blood. The ground is saturated with the Precious Blood! And yet it is not over! Fresh miscreants take the place of the now wearied executioners. Stripe is added to stripe, wound to wound, until the scourges tear away portions of the flesh itself, and the Saviour's body presents the appearance of having been flayed. Oh, my adorable Jesus! how dost Thou suffer for my sake! Alas! it is my sins which have bound Thee to the pillar. I bless Thee for Thine immense charity! Grant that such love and such anguish may not be lost upon me.

As I contemplate Thee, my beloved Lord, bathed in Thine own blood, Thy sacred flesh furrowed with stripes, Thy wounds become as so many voices which call upon me to love Thee. Compassion for Thy inhuman treatment has led many Saints to seek martyrdom. Holy persons have inflicted pain on their

bodies in memory of Thy terrible flagellation.
I cannot do this; but I cast myself at Thy
feet. I kiss the ground moistened by Thy
blood, and I offer Thee all the sufferings, great
and small, which it may please Thee to send
me, beseeching Thee to give me strength to
bear them, cheerfully and unrepiningly, in
memory of the anguish which Thou enduredst
in Thy scourging.

RESOLUTION.—I will, with God's grace, show
my gratitude for my Saviour's sufferings by
correcting the faults for which He suffered;
by overcoming my inclinations to anger, which
gave blows to His pure flesh; by conquering
my pride, for which He was humiliated; my
envy and jealousy, for which His body was
torn; my self-indulgence, for which His Blood
was shed.

PRAYER.—Sweet Jesus! wash me in Thy
Blood, I pray Thee, and, by the merits of Thy
cruel scourging, grant me forgiveness of my
sins, and grace to love Thee with my whole
heart.

THE CROWNING WITH THORNS.

"And the soldiers led Him into the court of the palace, and they called together the whole band; and they clothed Him with purple, and platting a crown of thorns, they put it upon Him. And they began to salute Him: Hail, king of the Jews. And they struck His head with a reed: and they did spit upon Him."
—St. Mark xv. 16—19.

INVOCATION.—My Blessed Jesus, teach me to love Thee more and more, as I meditate upon Thy sacred Passion.

I. The cruel scourging is over, but the Divine Sufferer is allowed no rest. "The soldiers led Him into the court of the palace, and they called together the whole band." The whole band! And Jesus is still alone, exposed to the ingenious ferocity of the troop of heathen soldiery.

They place Him upon a bench, and roughly tear off His clothes, causing the wounds made by the scourges to burst forth afresh. They throw an old purple cloak round His bruised shoulders, and in His hands they place a reed. Nor is this all. The mock king must be crowned. And so the brutal soldiers invent a kind of torture hitherto unheard of. They seize a handful of briars and weave them into a rude crown, interlacing them with a thorny plant of which the barbs are extremely sharp and long. I can hear the rough jests and coarse words which accompany the work.

Jesus sits patiently waiting, "blood-stained, dishonoured, wan, and pale, yet strangely pleasant to look on, and extremely gracious."

II. The soldiers "thrust a crown upon His head with rude vehemence. It is not round. It will not fit. They force the spikes into His skin, and the blood comes, blackly and slowly, and with excruciating pain. The Jews cheer these Romans in their barbarity; and one of them, not without loud, jocose applause, takes a heavy reed and beats the crown into the Sufferer's head. Long spikes go under the skin of the forehead and come out above the eyes. Others pierce His ears. Others fret against the nerves of His neck. Others penetrate the skull and burn like prickles of fire. He trembles from head to foot with the intolerable agony. His beautiful eyes are clouded with pain. His lips are bloodless with the extremity of endurance. But the face of a sleeping child is not more sweet than His, nor its heart more calm. He has grown more beautiful now that He is crowned."*

Our Blessed Lord has said that He is our Head and that we are His members. If, then,

* Faber. "Precious Blood," page 241.

we see our Head suffering thus, how ashamed should we be of our own cowardice in bearing pain! Will Jesus recognise me as His child, when He sees me wrapt up in myself, seeking, as I do, after comforts and ease and luxury?

A little pain in my face, a slight headache, is sufficient to call forth all my self-pity. I expect the compassion of others moreover, and think myself aggrieved if those around me do not strive to alleviate my discomfort. When shall I understand the beauty of suffering? When shall I comprehend the joy of having something to offer in union with the anguish of my Lord, exposed alone to the malice of a Roman cohort?

RESOLUTION.—I am determined, henceforth, to think less of my own ease, and to study the comfort of others before my own. I will also refrain from seeking after praise for my talents, or priding myself upon my intellectual acquirements, remembering that thorns pierced the head of Jesus on account of my pride and my self-love.

PRAYER.—Oh, my suffering Saviour! I pray Thee grant that I may never forget the torments which Thou didst endure for my sake. Make me love Thee and hate myself and everything which is capable of separating me from Thee.

JESUS GOES TO CALVARY.

"Then therefore he delivered Him to them to be crucified. And they took Jesus, and led Him forth. And bearing His own cross He went forth to that place which is called Calvary, but in Hebrew Golgotha."—St. John xix. 16, 17.

INVOCATION.—Jesus, for love of me Thou goest to Calvary. Oh, grant that I may live, suffer, and die with Thee.

I. Jesus is condemned to death. A vast multitude is assembled before Pilate's house. It is still early. A pale sun is struggling through the clouds. Occasional showers of sleet fall, whilst a chill, searching wind sweeps down from the neighbouring hills.

The Son of God comes forth, between two thieves, bearing His Cross. Executioners are on either side of Him, who torment Him in every imaginable way in order to incite the soldiery to insult him afresh. The procession is closed by a troop of armed men and the chief priests, and followed by a rabble composed of the scum of the populace. Jesus is led to His death like a meek lamb dragged to the slaughter. He is so exhausted from pain and loss of blood that He can scarcely stand. His sacred body is a mass of wounds. Blood trickles slowly from His thorn-crowned head.

His bruised shoulders are bent under the weight of a heavy wooden Cross. He moves feebly forward, His knees trembling and His body bent, and seeming as though every moment would be His last.

Where art Thou going, oh my Jesus, in such woful plight? "I am going to die for thee," the loving Saviour replies.

II. Twice He yields under the weight of His Cross, and falls with His face to the ground. The soldiers roughly drag Him to His feet. His condition is so pitiable that it provokes tears of compassion from the women of Jerusalem whom curiosity has brought to the spot. They weep over Jesus Whom they know not; and can my eyes remain dry? I follow Thee, my beloved Lord. The road is marked with Thy blood; Thy ruddy footprints will show me where Thy feet have passed, when I cannot approach Thee for the throng.

The way is long; the path leading to that green hill outside the city wall is steep. Jesus falls a third time. Oh, my sweetest Lord! how adorable art Thou in Thy weakness! I may take courage from these Thy falls, when I find myself weak, and beset by temptation to faint-heartedness. Thou, Who art strength itself, hast chosen to suffer from this human weakness, in order to console me when I fall—when I find my crosses heavy, and rebel and fret against them. Alas! too often I forget that it is only by the Way of the Cross that I can follow Thee; and I fall, not three, but a thousand times. Do thou, however, dear Lord, give me courage and strength to persevere, and change my aversion to crosses into love.

RESOLUTION.—I will make a practice of asking God daily to give me a love of suffering; and then, when sufferings come, instead of being surprised at their coming, it will seem quite natural to me that they should come.

PRAYER.—Blessed Mother! thou who hadst so great a share in the sufferings of thy Son, obtain for me the grace of loving Him and of suffering for Him.

JESUS MEETS HIS MOTHER.

"My grief hath overwhelmed me, my face is swollen with weeping, and my eyelids are sunk with heaviness."—Office B.V.M. Vesp. F. of the Seven Dolors.

INVOCATION.—Pray for me, oh most sorrowful Mother! I beseech thee, that I may be made worthy of the promises of Christ!

I. And the Mother of Jesus, where is she during the Passion of her beloved Son? Where is she at this dread hour in which her Beloved is drinking the cup of pain and humiliation to the dregs?

Mary is upon her knees in the house of Magdalen, to which she had retired when the Saviour quitted the Cenacle, in company with the other holy women.

She knows that the hour has come for her Son to be slain. How often in the tranquil days of Nazareth did He not explain to her the prophecies concerning Himself, and tell her of His future Passion, until every detail of its horrors was familiar to her mind. And now it has come to pass! The blows, the spittings, the flagellation, the crowning with thorns, all are present to the Mother; and as she shudderingly contemplates them in her mind, the sword predicted by Simeon is turned round and round, and deeper and deeper in her heart. She tried to gain admittance to the Prætorium and judgment hall, but was repulsed, and so she waits meekly in the house, trusting to St. John to bring her news of the dreadful scenes which are taking place.

II. At last he comes with the information that the sentence is passed, and that Jesus is going forth to die on the hill of Calvary. The brave Mother instantly determines to go out into the streets. She must see His face once more. St. John leads her tenderly round by a bye-way in order to escape the crowd, to a place where she will be able to see the dolorous procession as it passes.

Oh, my Mother! let me follow thee. I cannot leave thee on this sad day! I am not worthy of suffering with Jesus! Let me at least bear thee company on this thy Way of the Cross, and compassionate thy woe.

III. He comes! Behold Jesus bending under the weight of His ponderous Cross! The Mother sinks upon her knees, and stretches out her arms as Jesus comes up to her. "He halts for a moment. He lifts the one hand that is free, and clears the blood from His eyes. Is it to see her? Rather that she may see Him, His look of sadness, His look of love. She approaches to embrace Him. The soldiers thrust her rudely back. Oh, misery! and she is His Mother, too! For a moment she reeled with the push, and then again was still, her eyes fixed on His, His eyes fixed on hers. In a peace far beyond man's understanding she followed slowly on to Calvary: Magdalen and John beside themselves with grief, but feeling as if grace went out from her blue mantle, enabling them also to live with broken hearts."*

RESOLUTION.—I will strive to show my blessed Mother that I am not insensible to her sorrows by bearing patiently any crosses which her Divine Son may lay on my shoulders. I will take comfort from the sight of her affliction; and when I have any sorrows or afflictions I will take them to Mary's altar, and lay them at her feet, confident that her maternal heart will find pity and consolation for them all, and will give me strength to bear them meekly and even joyfully for the sake of Jesus.

PRAYER:

"Gentle Mother, we beseech thee,
By thy tears and trouble sore,
By the death of thy dear Offspring,
By the bloody wounds He bore,
Touch our hearts with that true sorrow
Which afflicted thee of yore."

---

* Faber, "Foot of the Cross," page 262.

THE CRUCIFIXION.

"And when they were come to the place which is called Calvary, they crucified Him there: and the robbers, one on the right hand, and the other on the left."—St. Luke xxiii. 33.

INVOCATION.—Queen of Martyrs, pray for us! who didst stand by the Cross of Christ.

I. The long, weary Way of the Cross is ended: Jesus has reached Calvary. Mary is there too. She beholds the brutal executioners throw Jesus down upon the Cross, after roughly stripping Him of His garments. She sees them nail His hands and feet; sees the quiver of pain which passes over His sacred limbs, without its once altering, by so much as a shade, the sweet look of peace which is upon His face, as He lies there on that cruel bed, His eyes upturned to heaven. Every blow of the hammer finds an echo in the Mother's heart.

II. "Now the Cross is lifted off from the ground with Jesus lying on it, the same sweet expression in His eyes, and is carried near to the hole which they have dug to receive the foot. They then fasten ropes to it, and, edging it to the brink of the hole, they begin to rear it perpendicularly by means of the ropes. When it is raised almost straight up, they work the foot of it gradually over the edge of the cavity, until it jumps into the socket with a vehement bound, which dislocates every bone, and nearly tears the body from the nails." (Faber, "Foot of the Cross," page 309.)

The three hours' agony begins before the Mother's eyes. Although it is mid-day, darkness creeps over the earth, the birds fly low, and their songs are hushed. The very animals coweringly seek shelter, and a nameless horror steals into the hearts of men.

The darkness deepens. There are fewer people near the Cross. All is silent. Mary draws nearer. St. John is at her side. Magdalen throws herself in an agony of grief upon the ground, clasping the foot of the Cross with her arms.

Oh, Mary! thou most afflicted of mothers! Who shall dare to describe thy woe? Thou seest the intolerable torments of thy Son, and thou art incapable of giving Him the least relief! Thou seest His lips parched with a burning thirst, and thou canst not moisten them! Thou canst not pillow His aching head upon thy bosom! His wounded body hangs suspended from three cruel nails, and thou canst not give its throbbing a moment's ease in thine arms, where, as a child, it has so often laid!

III. Seven times Jesus speaks. Seven times Mary hears the voice of her Beloved. As the last words, uttered with a loud cry, vibrate and die upon the still air, the suffering, thorn-crowned head droops towards the Mother standing below, the weary eyes close, and Jesus is dead!

Oh, wonderful Mother! Brave, loving Mother! Let me creep close to thee at this awful moment, when the very earth quakes and trembles. Shelter me in thy bosom, I entreat thee, and there let me weep with thee, for my heart is melted at the sight of thy desolation. Here, at the foot of the Cross, I beseech thee, sweet Mother, be with me at the hour of my death.

RESOLUTION.—I will try to prove my gratitude to Jesus by praying for the souls whom He died to save — the souls in Purgatory especially, in order that they may the sooner join their Saviour in Paradise. I will frequently say my Rosary for the suffering souls as I know that this devotion is specially pleasing to my Blessed Mother.

PRAYER.—Holy Mary, Mother of God, pray for us sinners, now and at the hour of our death.

THE TAKING DOWN FROM THE CROSS.

"And Joseph buying fine linen and taking Him down, wrapped Him up in the fine linen, and laid Him in a sepulchre which was hewn out of a rock. And he rolled a stone to the door of the sepulchre."—St. Mark xv. 46.

INVOCATION.—I adore Thee, Oh Christ! and I bless Thee, because by Thy holy Cross Thou hast redeemed the world.

I. The darkness of the eclipse has passed away. The sun is sinking like a ball of fire into the purple horizon. The little birds are joyously warbling their evensong, as the slanting rays cast a warm, red glow upon the group of mourners gathered round the Cross.

Mary still stands gazing up at the Body of her Son as it hangs white and lifeless upon the rugged wood. Her heart has been cruelly wounded by the last outrage which that Sacred Body suffered when the spear of the Roman soldier pierced the dead Heart of Jesus, and thence flowed a stream of blood and water. How weary the Mother must be! How exhausted with weeping and suffering!

II. The silence is broken anew by the sound of footsteps ascending the mount. It is Joseph of Arimathea and Nicodemus, both disciples of Our Lord. They approach the Blessed Virgin, and ask her permission to take down the body of Jesus, and lay it in a sepulchre in Joseph's garden.

See! with tenderest reverence they place a ladder against the Cross. Lovingly they detach the crown of thorns from the Blessed Head which it had so grievously tortured, and pass it down to Mary. Each nail, as it is loosened from the lacerated hands and feet, is silently placed in the Mother's lap. And now the body itself is lowered from the Cross. Mary is kneeling on the ground, her arms outstretched to receive her Son.

III. The Mother is seated at the foot of the Cross with the dead body of Jesus lying across her lap. "Ah, my Son!" I hear her lament, "what hast Thou done to Thy creatures that they should have maltreated Thee thus? Oh, cruel thorns! that they should have thus wounded Thee! Oh, nails! oh, lance! how could ye thus pierce the flesh of your Creator?" And Mary passes her hands gently and lovingly over the wounded brow. Fondly she smoothes the matted hair, and reads the traces of the Passion, scored in deep, livid seams over the lifeless Body. She tries to cross the outstretched arms upon the breast of Jesus, but they will not close, and Mary understands why they are so rigid. She understands that

Jesus wills that His arms shall remain ever opened wide, inviting the whole world to enter into His embrace.

IV. And now Mary must give up her dead Jesus into other hands to be borne to His tomb. The little party of mourners slowly and reverently descend the hill with their precious burthen, and lay the body of Him whom they loved in a new sepulchre, hewn out of the rock in Joseph's garden. They kneel and adore in silence, and then, tearfully, lingeringly, turn away from the grave.

RESOLUTION.—The afflicted Mother leaves her heart in the tomb with the body of Jesus. I will leave mine there also. I will remember that even there I may imitate my Divine Model. I must die to myself. He has said so. I must die to my faults, to my vanity, to my great love of pleasure. I will try and learn to be modest, humble, and charitable, and will practise some little privation every Friday in memory of the death of my Lord.

PRAYER. — My beloved Mother! By thy grief at parting with the Sacred Body of thy Divine Son, obtain for me, I beseech thee, forgiveness of all my sins, and grace to lead a hidden life.

MATER DESOLATA.

"O, all ye that pass by the way, attend and see if there be any sorrow like to my sorrow."—Lament. i. 12.

INVOCATION.—Holy Mary! Touch my heart with compassion, I pray thee. Let me share thy grief divine.

I. And now the childless Mother turns away from the Sepulchre. St. John and Magdalen are on either side of her, tenderly supporting her. Their path lies across Calvary. Oh, Mother! what a renewal of thy anguish! On reaching the Cross, Mary falls upon her knees and kisses the blood-stained wood, and then retraces the Way of the Cross into the guilty city—all its heart-rending scenes rising afresh before her mind. Wearily, feebly, she walks. Her head is covered by a veil, as though she were a newly made widow. Her countenance is so sad, so wan, so furrowed with weeping, that it excites the compassion of all who meet her.

Thus the Blessed Mother reaches the house of John—henceforth her home. *Home!* Can there ever be home for Mary without Jesus?

II. The long night has passed away. The sun is shining. Nature looks bright and fair. Earth wears no signs of the terrible deed which men have done. I enter the humble dwelling of St. John, to bring my loving compassion to my Mother's feet. She is seated there, meekly gazing towards Calvary. Her hands lie folded in her lap. She is calm and resigned. There is no violence in her grief. Her beautiful face, framed by the dark mourning-veil which covers her head, alone tells of the furnace of suffering through which she has passed. Her soft sweet eyes are dim with weeping, and every now and again I see a big tear roll slowly down her pale cheek. There is a look of peace upon her features which is almost an expression of hope.

The disciples visit her from time to time. Nicodemus also, and Joseph of Arimathea. I hear them speaking in low voices of the death of Jesus, of His holiness and of His sufferings, and grieving at His loss—but they do not give a thought to the oft-repeated promises of His resurrection.

Mary alone has "kept all these words in her heart." Her faith never falters. She believes that her Son will rise again, and therefore her broken heart lives on.

O Mother, I learn a touching lesson from thy calm, patient resignation! Our Blessed Lady does not add to the sorrows of the other mourners by any violent expression of her own. On the contrary, they are soothed and strengthened by the sight of her sweet patience. Even in common every-day life, occasions sometimes arise which make the hiding of my own feelings a duty. I am in trouble, perhaps; and my mother, or some one dear to me, is ill and must be spared the sight of my pain. Am I unselfish enough to be brave and to keep silence? Or it may be that duty, or charity, calls upon me to forego my habit of hearing daily Mass or Benediction. Do I make the sacrifice patiently and unrepiningly, without a shade on my face betraying that it is a sacrifice?

RESOLUTION.—I will endeavour to show my compassion for my afflicted Mother by deeds, and not words only. I will put my own feelings aside when those around me are suffering, and try to comfort and cheer them by my affectionate sympathy. I will try, with all my heart, to be unselfish, and to think of every-one before myself; and when God sends me sorrow and affliction, I will endeavour to bear my trouble patiently and unrepiningly, as our Blessed Lady bore hers, and not be a burthen to others.

PRAYER.—Suffering Heart of Mary, I beseech thee soften my heart, and give me a tender sympathy with the sorrows of my fellow-creatures.

ALLELUIA!

"He is risen!"—St. Matt. xxviii. 6.

INVOCATION.—O Lord Jesus, I beseech Thee, grant me a lively faith in Thy promises.

I. The following morning, at break of day, there is moving to and fro in the dwelling of the Mother of Jesus. Magdalen and the other holy women are preparing to carry precious perfumes and sweet spices to the Sepulchre, and I can imagine them kneeling for the Mother's blessing before they start on their holy errand.

Mary is now alone, absorbed in prayer. Her faith is as strong as ever, but her heart is sad. The separation from Jesus is intense suffering. Silent tears steal gently down her cheeks as she meekly prays, "Come back to me, my Son! Come back, my Beloved! Why dost Thou tarry?"

And as she thus touchingly laments, a soft light fills the room, and Mary hears the well-known voice of Jesus; its sweet tones no longer mournful and plaintive, as when they came down to her from the Cross, but joyous, exultant, and tender. She turns and beholds her Son. His countenance is radiant with Divine life. The Precious Blood is coursing once more through the veins which the Passion had drained, and a bright halo surrounds the Five Wounds, no longer lacerated and bleeding, but shining like roseate suns. Jesus has conquered death, and is risen. Alleluia! Alleluia!*

II. I prostrate myself with Mary at the feet of my Risen Lord! I bless Jesus with her mouth; for how can I thank Him worthily? How can I ever love Him enough? I rejoice with thee, my blessed Mother, in thy joy! How lovingly Mary gazes upon the face of Jesus! How tenderly she contemplates the ring left by the thorny crown around His gracious brow! Sorrow has passed away, and in her joy at beholding her Son once more, I can fancy that her past anguish is well-nigh forgotten!

If I am grateful to my Saviour for having died in order that I might live, the best way by which I can show Him my gratitude is by striving to make others share in the graces He is so anxious to bestow. I cannot go through the world persuading souls to love Christ. I cannot teach the heathen. I cannot preach. But I can always pray. Graces are abundant at Paschal-tide. Jesus is asking to be received

* The apparition of Our Blessed Lord to his Mother on Easter morning has been handed down to the faithful by the Fathers of the Church.

into the hearts of men. He is waiting in the Tabernacle, longing to come forth. I can help souls by praying for their conversion. I can pray that those who are about to make their Easter-duties may receive Jesus worthily. I can pray that the lips of the priest may become more and more eloquent and persuasive.

There are others who have not the same advantages as myself. I might tell them about the sweet Saviour Who died upon a Cross for them. I might help them to know Him and to love Him, by lending them books, giving them holy pictures, showing them that I love them for His sake, and so win their hearts to Him by my own poor kindness.

RESOLUTION.—I will make a practice of performing certain acts of devotion every Easter, in order that hesitating souls may be brought to Confession and Communion, and will say special prayers for the intention of the Confessors who are trying to convert sinners. I will, moreover, endeavour to help souls by setting a good example of piety and devotion to Holy Church.

PRAYER.—My adorable Saviour! I love Thee with my whole heart. Never permit me to separate myself from Thee again. Make me love Thee more and more, and then do with me what Thou wilt.

ASCENSION OF OUR BLESSED LORD.

"And it came to pass whilst He blessed them, He departed from them, and was carried up into heaven."
—St. Luke xxiv. 51.

INVOCATION.—Sweet Saviour, who didst rise again from the dead, give me a great desire of heaven, I entreat Thee.

I. For forty days Jesus Risen has dwelt upon the earth, appearing, now to His blessed Mother, now to the holy women, now to one or two of the Apostles, now to all the disciples assembled together, giving them constant proofs of His resurrection and of His love. The charity and humility of the Saviour shine forth more sweetly than ever in this His condescension. After such a death as His, after His abandonment and betrayal by His disciples, He comes back to them with renewed proofs of His love. He will not leave His chosen flock until their faith is quite firm, until their love is perfect.

Oh, Jesus! I adore Thee! I kneel at Thy feet. I gaze upon Thy glorified countenance. It is the same Jesus indeed. Here are the marks of the nails! There is the wound made by the cruel spear! Oh, my beloved Lord! I thank Thee for showing me Thy Sacred Heart, opened wide to compassionate my misery!

Thou hast been wounded for my sins, therefore Thou wilt never refuse to listen to me, when I come to Thee humble and repentant. Give me more faith and more love, I entreat Thee.

II. The disciples are together in the Cenacle at Jerusalem. The Mother of Jesus, Magdalen, and the other holy women are there also. Suddenly the Saviour appears in their midst. He takes His place amongst them for the last time—no longer in order to give them a proof of His Resurrection, but as a last mark of affection before ascending to His Heavenly Father. The words of Jesus are solemn. I watch the Apostles hang with rapt, reverent attention upon His lips, as He gives them their mission to go forth and convert all nations in His Name.

III. And now the moment of separation is at hand. Jesus rises. Once more I follow my Lord as He descends from Mount Sion and directs His steps towards the Mount of Olives. This time it is morning. The sun is shining brightly. All Nature is resplendent, and seems to rejoice in the presence of her Creator. Jesus is followed by His Mother, by the holy women and disciples, in all one hundred and twenty persons. Once more He walks through the streets dyed with His Blood, this time invisible to the inhabitants of the guilty city. What a glorious procession!

IV. It is mid-day when Jesus arrives at the summit of the mountain. I watch Him reverently, as He pauses a moment, looking lovingly upon His blessed Mother and the little company of the faithful around her. And then He raises His hands, and they fall upon their knees. Jesus blesses them, and as He blesses, His feet are raised from the ground, and He ascends towards heaven. Mary and the others remain upon their knees watching the beloved Form in adoring silence until a cloud envelopes Jesus and hides Him from their sight. Tears fall from the eyes of those who are left, but they are tears of joy as well as of sadness.

And now that my Lord has ascended into heaven, what lesson must I take home with me from the sacred mountain? I must take home a great longing to be with Jesus. A great desire of heaven must fill my heart. My place is already marked out in those celestial courts. The way to reach it may be long and fatiguing, but I have the footprints of Jesus to guide me, I have the Sacraments to strengthen me, my Blessed Mother to console me when I am weary, a guardian-angel to hold me up when I stumble, the example of the Saints to encourage me to persevere, and graces awaiting me at every step.

RESOLUTION.—Courage then! I will not fear! If Jesus has trodden the path of my earthly pilgrimage, He knows all its difficulties, and He will have pity on my weakness. I will place my feet in His Divine footprints and press bravely forward, confident that He sees and blesses my efforts.

PRAYER.—Oh, my beloved Saviour! grant that I may follow Thee faithfully. Draw me so powerfully towards Thee that I may never lose Thy grace. Be Thou the rule of my thoughts, desires, and affections, so that my life may be holy and entirely consecrated to Thee, and I may imitate, as far as be possible to my poor feeble nature, the Divine example which Thou didst show me whilst on earth for my sake.

MAY THE MOST DIVINE HEART OF JESUS AND THE MOST PURE HEART OF MARY BE KNOWN, PRAISED, BLESSED, LOVED, HONOURED, AND GLORIFIED ALWAYS AND IN ALL PLACES. AMEN.

www.ingramcontent.com/pod-product-compliance
Lightning Source LLC
Chambersburg PA
CBHW030107170426
43198CB00009B/529